For my late parents and grandmother,
whom I miss dearly.

BEE YINN LOW

Easy Chinese Recipes

FAMILY FAVORITES
FROM DIM SUM TO KUNG PAO

foreword by Jaden Hair

TUTTLE Publishing

Tokyo | Rutland, Vermont | Singapore

Pork and Chive Dumplings

Variety of Produce

Vendors in San Francisco Chinatown

Scrambled Eggs with Shrimp

Contents

Vendor in Los Angeles Chinatown

Crispy Pan-fried Noodles

Shopping in Chinatown

Green Onions (Scallions)

Mongolian Beef

Sichuan String Beans

Chinese Eggplant

Okra and Chinese Chives

Foreword by Jaden Hair

I am absolutely thrilled that you're holding this cookbook, because that means you'll be discovering the secrets to authentic Chinese home cooking. I'm also delighted because you'll have a chance to get to know one of my very favorite "blog-sisters," Bee Yinn Low, and her kitchen stories.

Bee and I first met just about four years ago, when I first started blogging at *SteamyKitchen.com*. Back then we were a little shy online (and a little cautious), keeping our real names on the back-burner. Everyone called her "Rasa" and I was "Steamy" and you can imagine the funny looks we would get when inadvertently referring to ourselves by our blog names in real life situations.

The anonymity soon gave way to the discovery of our mutual passions, not just for Asian cuisine, but figuring out how to turn a fun, little hobby blog into a successful business and making it the best job ever.

We'd spent late nights on the phone talking SEO, Wordpress, CSS and HTML. There was so much to share and learn, and if you can imagine two grown women giggling about a new plugin, well, you can pretty much call us soul sisters.

We started trickling family stories into our conversations and it wasn't before long that I realized that I knew more about Bee and her family than I did some of my neighbors, even though she was in California and I was in Florida, and we had never met in person. At our first meeting we were like little chatty, giggly schoolgirls, it was non-stop talking. Bee is like a sister to me, she's the first person I turn to when I have a cooking question about Chinese food or when my blog breaks down.

She's a generous, happy spirit, and I think you'll experience that on each and every page of this book.

Happy Cooking,

Jaden Hair

Jaden Hair, author of *The Steamy Kitchen Cookbook*
SteamyKitchen.com

Honey Walnut Shrimp

Baby G

Baby G, 5 Weeks Old

Shopping in Chinatown

Author's Preface

Words can't begin to describe how elated I am to be the author of this book. Writing a cookbook has always been a dream of mine, and I can't help but feel utterly blessed, humbled, and above all, thankful, to have such a wonderful opportunity.

This cookbook has been a labor of love. I worked on it during the pregnancy of my beloved son—one of the most exhilarating and life-changing phases of my life. What you are holding now is indeed other baby—my culinary baby—one that I had carried alongside my adorable baby G.

This cookbook is a compilation of my favorite recipes: Chinese classics, all-time favorites, dim sum, dumplings, and more. Some recipes reflect my many travels in Asia, especially in China and Hong Kong. Others are my interpretation of popular Chinese dishes, perfected through years of preparing them at home. A selected few were passed on to me by my friends, who firmly believe that great recipes are to be shared and enjoyed.

Reading through this beautiful cookbook, I know that my family—G, baby G, my aunt, uncle, siblings and the entire family back home in Malaysia—and my beloved ones, dear friends, loyal fans and readers of Rasa Malaysia (http://rasamalaysia.com) will be exceedingly proud of me and this accomplishment.

Thank you ever so much for your support. I hope you use and enjoy the recipes in this cookbook and I wish you all "Happy Cooking!"

Bee Yinn Low

Bee Yinn Low
RasaMalaysia.com

Growing Up in a Chinese Family

Someone once asked me: What is your favorite sound in the world?

"The sizzling sound of Chinese food, when the ingredients are added into a hot wok and that distinct aroma fills the kitchen."

I grew up listening to the musical rhythms of Chinese cooking in my home. Even though I was born in Penang, Malaysia, with a Nyonya (local Chinese in the Malay Peninsula who have adopted local traditions) grandmother, I am, ultimately, Chinese. I grew up eating mostly Chinese food, speaking a Chinese dialect as my mother tongue, and attending Chinese school until college. My late mother was the designated cook in our family; watching her cook was a significant part of my childhood. As a little girl, there was something inherently attractive about what was going on in the kitchen.

Every morning, my mother headed out to the local market, scouring the stands and vendors for the freshest ingredients. Upon her return, she would be busy with the preparation work: shelling shrimp, cleaning fish, cutting vegetables, chopping chicken, or slicing meat. I would always stand beside my mother, sometimes on tiptoe, watching silently and curiously as she proceeded with her daily kitchen chores. The motions and sequences danced in front of my eyes—I was mesmerized.

The first round of cooking would always start just after 11 a.m., when my mother would fire up her dark, well-seasoned Chinese wok on the propane stovetop. As soon as a swirl of white smoke began to appear from the edges of the wok, she would pour in some peanut oil. Then the nutty aroma of peanut oil started wafting out of the wok. Chopped garlic or ginger (depending on the dish she was making) and the main ingredient would be added into the wok, and that was when the loud and lively sizzling sound of the wok started to sound like a seductive song. Then the unforgettable fragrance of Chinese cooking permeated our home.

This is how I learned to love Chinese food.

Shopping at the Asian Market

Learning to Cook Chinese

While I was an ardent observer of my mother's cooking, I never had a chance to actually practice the cooking part because my mother wouldn't allow it.

"You don't know how to cook. You would just spoil everything," she would say in a disapproving tone.

I was allowed to help her with the prepping of the ingredients, such as the mundane chore of removing roots from heaps of fresh bean sprouts, but my opportunity to create these dishes wouldn't come until later. In fact, it was not until I left home to attend college in Kuala Lumpur—the capital of Malaysia—that I had my first real opportunity to cook: a potluck party hosted by me. The menu I planned was a classic array of Chinese dishes: stir-fry vegetables, soup, shrimp, and chicken—guaranteed to impress...so I thought.

After years of observation, I was convinced that Chinese cooking was easy. Instead, my stir-fried vegetables turned a horrid purple due to over-cooking; the soup was bland and dull; the shrimp didn't taste good; and the chicken was salty and rubbery. Still, dinner had to be served and so everyone sat around the table silently eating, and then someone sighed (in relief, I think), "I am so glad that dinner's over!"

I was thoroughly embarrassed, but it was true, I was a TERRIBLE cook. I thought I had "training" while growing up, but my lack of experience was obvious. Watching my mother cook hadn't created cooking skills, I learned that good cooking needs to be cultivated and earned—a cook's journey that I had to undertake for myself.

Soon after that I got a hold of my first Chinese "cookbook," a recipe booklet, distributed with the purchase of a bottle of oyster sauce. This booklet covered the fundamentals of Chinese cooking and some of the different cooking methods involved in Chinese cooking. I studied the recipes earnestly, and for the first time, I started grasping the basics: how to cook meat to velvety tenderness, how to ensure that vegetables are crisp, and how the seasonings need to complement and balance the natural flavors of the ingredients. I followed the booklet's recipes, went through my share of trials and errors, and soon after that I started cooking Chinese food successfully. I produced aromatic and mouthwatering ginger and scallion chicken—one of the classic Chinese stir-fry dishes. I made restaurant-style sweet-and-sour shrimp with the robust flavors that intermingled with the succulence and texture of the shrimp.

My Late Parents in Yosemite

I served glossy green vegetables with oyster sauce that were crisp and crunchy.

As I started to master the art of fundamental Chinese cooking, my creations started to get unanimous nods and praises from my family and friends, marking the defining moment in which I had blossomed into a good cook. It was also then that I became a die-hard aficionado of Chinese cuisine, a cuisine that I have resolved to continue learning about, experimenting with, and, of course, eating!

Over the ensuing years, I was fortunate to have had many opportunities to travel all over Asia, especially to China and Hong Kong. With each journey, I discovered and experienced something new about Chinese cuisine. In the small alleys of Beijing's *hutong*, I sampled brightly flavorful *jiaozi* and dumplings, and reveled in freshly made noodles and soups. In a 1930's era mansion in Shanghai's French Concession, I savored impeccable and refined Shanghainese cuisine. At a roadside stall in Chengdu, Sichuan, my taste buds were treated to the explosively flavorful, tongue-numbing, lip-tingling spicy *mala* Sichuan concoctions. In a fine Cantonese restaurant in Hong Kong, I was immersed in a gastronomical ecstasy after a 10-course Cantonese banquet dinner of supreme delicacies. On the island of Xiamen, in the Fujian province, I was treated to an array of delectable seafood dishes that were remarkably succulent and tasty. This amazing cuisine is a culinary celebration of gastronomical variety in both texture and taste making it my favorite cuisine in the world.

Basic Cooking Techniques and Tips

Chinese cooks place a heavy emphasis on basic cooking techniques and tips. In fact, they are as important as the recipes—a great recipe might turn into a complete failure without proper execution during the preparation and cooking process. This chapter covers some basic Chinese cooking techniques and kitchen tips that I have learned from professional chefs, my late mother, and other experienced home cooks. These are my golden rules for making scrumptious Chinese food at home.

How to Tenderize Meat

This technique is best used for chicken breast, which is usually dry, coarse, and chewy. For the illustration here I use chicken breast, but this technique also works for beef and pork. If you already have a tender cut of beef, this technique is not necessary unless you want the texture to be silky smooth like the ones served at Chinese restaurants. If you like the natural meaty taste of beef, please also take note that this technique will result in losing that beefy flavor.

8 oz (250 g) chicken breast
1 teaspoon baking soda

1 Cut or slice the chicken breast per the recipe instruction. Make sure it's cut or sliced into uniform pieces.
2 Mix the baking soda with the chicken. Make sure the chicken breast is evenly coated with the baking soda. Set aside for 15 minutes.
3 Place the chicken in a colander and rinse thoroughly with cold running water. Rinse a few times if desired. Pat dry with paper towels. The chicken is now ready for the marinade or whatever preparation is called for in the recipe.

TENDERIZING MEAT Texture is a highly prized component in Chinese cooking, especially when it comes to proteins. Meat—especially chicken, pork, or beef—is always cooked so that the result is a silky-smooth mouthfeel that is succulent and tender, with a glossy sheen. Traditionally, velveting is a technique used in professional and home kitchens for tenderizing meat. Meats are cut into uniform pieces, coated with an egg white and starch mixture, and then cooked to the desired satiny consistency. A few years ago, I learned a quick tip from a Chinese chef, who uses baking soda as the secret ingredient in his restaurant. He taught me the following technique, and I have been producing the most amazing, tender, and juicy stir-fried meats at home ever since. Baking soda, or sodium bicarbonate, is an alkaline agent at pH8.2. As such, it neutralizes the acids and breaks down the proteins in the meat and therefore makes a superb tenderizer. Another plus, it also acts as a deodorizer to rid the meat of any potential foul smell it might have. If you are skeptical about using baking soda in home cooking, please don't be because it's an essential ingredient in baking. My technique calls for baking soda as a "dry rub," it's rinsed off thoroughly before cooking. Of course, this meat tenderizing process is optional, so it's up to you. However, if you want to impress your family or guests with perfectly tender, smooth, and succulent meat, here is how you can do it.

How to Cut Beef Against the Grain

Examine and identify the direction of the muscle or the grain on the beef carefully. The grain will run in one direction. Using a cleaver or sharp knife, slice the beef crosswise, or against the grain, into bite-sized slices. Personally, I get the best results when I cut or slice the beef at a slightly slanted angle. This ensures that I get a bigger piece of the tender, soft, and melt-in-your-mouth meat after it is cooked. It makes a big difference, so do not slice or cut the beef parallel to the grain or you might get a piece of meat that's as tough as jerky after cooking.

CUTTING BEEF Have you ever wondered why the same cut of beef would yield a completely different texture if cut incorrectly? Cutting or slicing beef against the grain is a basic technique that a home-cook should learn. The difference is tender and juicy beef versus rubbery and chewy beef. Cutting beef against the grain is the most critical step in preparing beef dishes.

How to Make Your Shrimp "Bouncy"

8 oz (250 g) shelled and deveined shrimp
1 teaspoon baking soda
1 tablespoon egg white
½ tablespoon tapioca starch (preferred) or cornstarch
1 cup ice cubes

1 Rub and massage the baking soda on the shrimp and put in a bowl. Add cold water until the shrimp is submerged. Add the ice cubes to the water. Set aside for 30 minutes.
2 Place the shrimp in a colander and rinse thoroughly with cold running water. Rinse a few times if desired. Pat dry with paper towels.
3 Add the egg white and starch to the shrimp and mix well. Leave the shrimp in the refrigerator for at least 4–6 hours or best overnight. You will notice that the flesh of the shrimp firms up and becomes denser. The shrimp is now ready for use.

"BOUNCY" SHRIMP Have you ever had Chinese shrimp dishes or dim sum where the shrimp are so crisp and crunchy that they literally "bounce" in your mouth? In Chinese, this revered texture is called *"shuang cui."*

My uncle told me that Cantonese chefs—especially those specializing in dim sum—treat and drain their shrimp with cold running tap water (water massage) for hours, which eventually results in that dense and bouncy texture that we all love. This technique certainly works but it's not sensible for a home kitchen because gallons of water will be wasted.

After extensive research and many conversations with Chinese chefs and restaurateurs, I eventually came up with the technique that delivers a satisfactory result for home cooks. Again, the secret ingredient is baking soda, which is used to treat the shrimp before they are coated with an egg white and tapioca starch or cornstarch mixture, a process my Chinese chef friend, Mr. Wong, called *"shang jiang."*

As most shrimp sold in the United States are previously frozen, I find this technique rewarding when I make shrimp dumplings, dim sum, or Shrimp Wonton Soup (page 56). If the shrimp you get lacks the bouncy texture, use the steps (see left) in recipes where the perfect mouthfeel of the shrimp is highly desired. Please take note that this process is time consuming, so it's an optional step.

Deep-frying Tips and Tricks

Everyone loves the golden-glory of perfectly fried foods—crispy, crunchy, yet tender and moist on the inside. Ironically, deep-frying is probably one of the most dreaded cooking methods. It's also one of those kitchen techniques shunned by home cooks, including the experienced ones. Many people are afraid of deep-frying mostly because of the hot and splattering oil, which everyone has experienced at some point in their cooking life. Those who are not familiar with how to control the heat of the oil will risk ruining a dish. Here are my tips and tricks that make deep-frying easier and a lot less intimidating.

1 The perfect temperature for deep-frying is between 300°F (150°C)—360°F (180°C). Deep-frying within this range of temperature will make sure that foods are cooked properly—the outside of the food will be browned evenly while the inside remains tender and juicy. The deep-fried food will become crispy but not excessively greasy. The oil penetration is confined to the surface of the food and the moisture content of the ingredient is not lost. I always deep-fry at 350°F (175°C).

2 If the oil temperature is over 360°F (180°C), it might be too hot because the outside of the food will overcook quickly but the inside will be undercooked. Turn down the heat or add more oil to lower the temperature.

3 If you don't have a thermometer, use visual cues. One visual cue is when the oil is ready for deep-frying, you will see small oil bubbles continue to float towards the surface of the oil and a faint haze will appear. You can also use a pair of wooden chopsticks to test readiness by dipping the chopsticks in the oil and as soon as bubbles form, it's heated enough for deep-frying.

4 Don't skimp on oil. For the best results, the oil should cover and submerge the fried food. Ideally, the oil level should be at least 2 inches (5 cm) above the food.

5 Pat dry the ingredient before deep-fry-ing. Food with excessive moisture or water is the number one reason for splattering. You can use a large stockpot (instead of a wok or stir-fry pan) for deep-frying. A deep stockpot can help prevent excessive splattering.

6 If you are deep-frying food coated with a wet batter, add some oil into the batter before deep-frying. The oil helps loosen up the food so it doesn't clump and stick together. Want extra crispy battered foods? Increase the temperature of the oil and return the food into the wok or stockpot and deep-fry a second time.

7 If there's too much food in the oil, the temperature will drop significantly and the result will be soggy and greasy food. So it's best to deep-fry in batches.

8 Remove the fried food with a strainer or slotted spoon and drain the excess oil by placing it on a wire rack. Alternatively, you can also place the food in a dish lined with paper towels.

9 Some foods tend to cause splattering regardless of moisture content, so use the wok lid or stockpot cover to fend off any potential splattering.

10 After deep-frying, transfer the oil to an airtight container after it completely cools down. You can reuse the oil but repeated usage will cause the oil to darken or turn rancid leaving an unpleasant smell and taste. Discard the frying oil after using it 2 or 3 times.

Perfect Stir-frying Techniques

Stir-frying is one of the fundamental techniques of successful Chinese cooking, one that you ought to master if you wish to make Chinese food at home. Here are my quick techniques and tips for perfect everyday stir-frying.

1 The wok or skillet must be fully heated before stir-frying. You'll know if the wok or skillet has reached the optimum heat when a swirl of white smoke starts appearing on its surface.

2 Add the oil after the wok or skillet is fully heated. Make sure that the oil completely coats the bottom surface of the wok or skillet.

3 Cut the ingredients, such as chicken, beef, pork, or seafood, into uniform pieces. Also, it's very important to have all the ingredients prepared, measured, and placed close to the wok or skillet. Once in the wok or skillet, spread the ingredients in one layer to ensure even cooking.

4 Stir-fries are generally prepared with a light sauce. Mix the sauce in advance in a small bowl by combining all the ingredients in the sauce. If cornstarch is used, make sure that it's completely dissolved. Before adding the sauce into the stir-fry, quickly stir the sauce one last time to ensure that nothing settled at the bottom of the bowl. An authentic Chinese stir-fry dishes shouldn't be doused in too much sauce; the sauce should barely cling to the ingredients.

5 The spatula should play an active role in stir-frying. Use it to continuously stir and toss the ingredients in a back and forth, circular, turning, and/or flipping motions.

Basic Tools and Utensils

Believe it or not, I don't have a big kitchen at home. Living in a small townhome, I have limited counter, working, and storage spaces in my kitchen (no kitchen island for sure!). So when it comes to basic tools and utensils for Chinese cooking, I use only the essentials—electronic rice cooker, wok, spatula, Chinese cleaver, bamboo steamers, etc. Living in a typical American home, with a smoke detector planted right above my kitchen, I also have a stir-fry pan that I use alongside my two woks because the intense heat from the wok sets off the smoke alarm every two days! Nonetheless, there is one thing I can't complain about in my kitchen: I have a gas range, which is superb for Chinese stir-frying and cooking.

Here is the list of basic tools and utensils for making delicious Chinese food at home.

Bamboo Steamers I love making dim sum and dumplings at home so I have stocked up on traditional Chinese bamboo steamers of various sizes: large, medium, and small. My favorite would be the 6-inch bamboo steamers that nestle comfortably in my wok, plus the smaller steamer that always reminds me of my enjoyable dim sum experiences at a Chinese restaurant.

The size of the bamboo steamer is a personal preference, but do make sure that you get the ones that would fit perfectly in your wok or stir-fry pan (your cooking pan should be approximately 2–3 inches wider than the bamboo steamers). If you buy smaller bamboo steamers, buy at least two baskets so you can stack them up and steam more food. If you get a bigger size, say a 12-inch bamboo steamer, one basket should be sufficient.

Please take note that the bamboo steamer should sit at least 1–2 inches above the boiling water inside the wok and the domed lid should be closed tightly to allow the food to steam efficiently. For cleaning, simply scrub and rinse the bamboo steamers with water.

Chinese Strainer or Slotted Spoon A traditional Chinese strainer with a bamboo handle and wire/steel mesh always reminds me of street vendors who use it to quickly drain and shake off the excess water from boiled noodles. In my kitchen, I use the strainer for a couple of purposes: scooping and draining food after deep-frying and removing blanched foods from boiling water.

Chinese-style strainers—both traditional and modern—can be found at Asian supermarkets or kitchen supply stores. If you can't find them, western-style slotted spoon with extra generous scoop size will also work.

Clay Pot Also called a "sand pot," most clay pots have a sandy and coarse exterior, with a glazed and smooth dark brown interior for cooking. The clay pot is a great utensil for stewing and braising because of its ability to retain heat. It commonly comes in three different sizes: big, medium, and small. A medium sized clay pot is big enough for most Chinese clay pot cooking recipes. Foods cooked in a clay pot are usually served as is, meaning, you can just eat directly from the pot. After use, the clay pot can be washed with just warm water (using soap is not recommended).

Cleaver When my late parents came to visit us in 2000, the first thing that my mother bought me was a Chinese cleaver. She didn't like my "western-style" knives. The Chinese cleaver is just as versatile as a wok, it's used for an array of kitchen tasks: slicing, cutting, dicing, shredding, chopping, peeling, pounding, and mincing. My mother had such great cleaver skills that she even used it as a can opener!

The Chinese cleaver might appear intimidating because of the large blade but it's such a nifty tool once you get over the initial apprehension because of its size and appearance. I use a Chinese cleaver on a daily basis—the very same one that my mother bought me, which now holds great sentimental value.

Cutting Board A cleaver would have no place in the kitchen without a proper cutting board. A cutting board is one of the most vital tools in the kitchen. Without a cutting board, prepping would be almost impossible. While I grew up watching my late mother working on her old wooden cutting board made from a tree stump, my preferred cutting boards are those made of bamboo. I have one that I have

been using for many years—it's hygienic, easy to clean, sturdy, heavy, and doesn't slip off a wet counter top like those white plastic cutting boards. Also, it doesn't get scratched easily so the likelihood of uncooked food sticking on the surface almost never happens.

Rice Cooker The rice cooker is an indispensable tool for Chinese cooking. Of course, you can make perfect boiled rice with your gas or electric range, but a rice cooker is so efficient and a great time-saver.

A rice cooker is compact and fits just about anywhere on your kitchen countertop, as long as it's close to the electric outlet. The biggest virtue is that a rice cooker makes perfect, fluffy, and soft rice every single time and the "Keep Warm" function guarantees moist and heated rice anytime of the day!

My favorite brand of rice cooker is Zojirushi. They are not cheap, but it's worth investing in a high-quality rice cooker

because, trust me, you will only ever need one! Zojirushi rice cookers come with a thicker nonstick inner cooking pan that is durable, easy to clean, and does not get easily scratched. The menu is also quite simple to use and very intuitive.

Wok, Stir-fry Pan, or Skillet The Chinese wok is a distinguished utensil in the kitchen because of its versatility. It's used for stir-frying, deep-frying, steaming, boiling, blanching, braising, stewing, and smoking—it's an all-purpose tool for a wide spectrum of Chinese cooking styles. A Chinese wok is also a kitchen tool that you want to use and keep for a long time as the glorious patina builds over time, which essentially "coats" the wok with a nonstick layer.

There are two kinds of woks: cast iron and carbon steel. In my kitchen, I use both a pre-seasoned 14-inch lightweight cast iron wok by Wok Star (http://wokstar.us) as well as a carbon steel wok. I also have a high quality stir-fry pan, which I use for braising and stewing and other dishes that don't require intense heat. It's undeniable that the best and most refined Chinese dishes are cooked with a wok, but you can use a stir-fry pan for all the recipes in this cookbook. The biggest difference between a wok and a stir-fry pan is the nonstick coating on the stir-fry pan, which is user-friendly, especially for beginners to wok cooking. The nonstick surface also means that there is no need for the seasoning. The main downside for using a stir-fry pan versus a traditional wok

Wok and Wok Cover

is that a regular nonstick stir-fry pan is not recommended for intense high heat and hence it's very hard to produce *wok hei* or "the breath of wok," which is highly prized in Chinese cooking. To learn more about wok cooking, I recommend Grace Young's books: *The Breath of Wok* and *Stir-frying to the Sky's Edge*.

Most American homes are well equipped with skillets, which is a good substitute for a wok or stir-fry pan. However, do take note that skillets have a flat surface and are pretty shallow, so food tends to spill out because of that. The flat surface also makes tossing and stirring more cumbersome than a wok or stir-fry pan. Ultimately though, I highly recommend using a wok for Chinese cooking, but choose the utensil that you feel most comfortable using. You can always start with a nonstick stir-fry pan or skillet and then upgrade to a Chinese wok once you are comfortable with stir-frying and cooking Chinese food.

Wok Cover or Stir-Fry Pan Lid I love my wok cover as much as my wok. Wok covers work hand-in-hand with the wok and the lightweight aluminum body is so easy to handle. It's particularly helpful to fend off the splattering oil, especially when you add wet ingredients into the wok—such as rinsed vegetables or tofu still dotted with water. For stewing and braising, wok covers work wonders in keeping the ingredients moist and tender during the cooking process. Most stir-fry pans come with a glass lid, which serves the same function, but these are heavier. If you buy the wok cover and stir-fry pan lid separately, remember to measure the diameter of your wok or stir-fry pan so the cover fits correctly.

Wok Mitt I feel obliged to add the wok mitt to this chapter because it's such a handy and practical tool when it comes to wok cooking. A mitt is especially useful if you don't have a wok ring because

you can secure and stabilize the wok by holding onto one of the handles. I have had too many incidents where I've burned my hand while cooking. Now that I use a mitt at least my left hand is protected from splattering.

Wok Ring If you have a regular residential gas or electric range in your kitchen, your round-bottom wok or stir-fry pan will probably wobble every time you use it. To stabilize the wok or stir-fry pan, you can get a wok ring that sits on the gas or electric range that cradles your wok or stir-fry pan snuggly.

Spatula There are a few types of spatula: steel, wood, plastic, rubber or silicone. Personally, I am a big fan of the Chinese steel spatula, which is perfect for a wok. The thin and slightly curved steel surface is great for stirring, tossing, and flipping during cooking. It also works marvelously for shoveling and scooping out the food when it's cooked.

If you have a nonstick stir-fry pan, I recommend using a wood or plastic spatula to avoid scratching the nonstick surface. A wood or plastic spatula is thicker, so it's a little clumsier to use, especially when you are trying to get beneath the food. My hubby refuses to use a wood or plastic spatula because he can't flip his breakfast omelet with it! I don't recommend rubber or silicon spatula because it's just about impossible to use it in the wok or stir-fry pan. They are too pliable for the continuous stirring and tossing motions of Chinese stir-frying.

(page 14)(page 15)(page 110)

THE DIFFERENT USES OF A CHINESE WOK

If there is only one Chinese utensil that you wanted to invest in your kitchen, it's probably a Chinese wok. Wok is a magical utensil because of its many uses and versatility. In my kitchen, I use it for almost everything: stir-frying, deep-frying, steaming, boiling, blanching, and braising. Here are my quick tips of using wok other than basic stir-frying (page 14) and deep-frying (page 15).

STEAMING Add water to the wok and use a bowl to prop up the steamed dish. Make sure that the water level is enough to generate the hot steam but not too much. I usually leave at least 1-inch (2.5 cm) of gap between the water and the steamed dish, which is propped up on a bowl. After steaming, discard the water from the wok and pat dry with paper towels. Do not leave any traces of water in the wok as it might become rusty.

BOILING I often use my wok to make soup or to boil eggs. It's really convenient and delivers great results. Make sure that you wash off the residue on the wok and pat the wok surface dry to avoid rusting.

BLANCHING When making vegetable dishes such as Chinese Broccoli with Oyster Sauce (page 110), wok is a great tool for quick blanching of the vegetables. Add a few drops of oil into the water and bring it to boil. Drop the vegetables into the wok and remove immediately with a strainer or slotted spoon as soon as the vegetables become wilted or cooked.

BRAISING Wok is great for braising, especially meat dishes. Use the wok lid to cover the ingredients in the wok and turn the heat to medium or low to allow the meat to cook through. Perfectly braised meat should be tender and deeply flavorful with bone-in meat falling off the bones.

Seasoning a Cast Iron Wok by Wok Star Eleanor Hoh of www.wokstar.us

This seasoning method is ONLY for a Chinese, round bottom cast iron wok with two cast iron handles (the best for successful wok cooking.) When new, cast iron woks have a gray coating that must be removed. Seasoning is the most important procedure to set up your wok; it prevents the wok from rusting and gives it an overall protection. A simple explanation of "seasoning" means using heat to open the pores of the wok so the oil gets absorbed into the pores. When seasoning is done correctly, the wok will look bronze and black. With frequent use, a coating (patina) will build and becomes a natural "non-stick" surface and will turn pitch black, which is what you want. You need to season your wok only once but it can be "reseasoned" if necessary. (See below under Care and Maintenance of Your Wok.)

In Asia, typically the wok is seasoned with aromatics only on the inside. This requires constant stir-frying to make sure seasoning has occurred all around the wok—this is hard work. I use a much easier two-step process. Simply baking the wok to open the pores makes seasoning the interior much easier!

You need a little time and patience. Open doors and windows and blast the fan to blow out the smoke. Please be careful of grease fires and have a fire extinguisher at the ready. If you are sensitive to smoke, wear a mask and glasses. When washing the wok the first time gray discoloration may occur.

Directions for Seasoning Your Wok

1 Preheat oven to 300°F (150°C). Have all your tools ready. Wash the inside and outside of the wok, with hot soapy water and a stainless steel scourer (this includes the handles). This is a very important step: Scrub till you stop seeing a gray color in the water but not so hard that it's bare metal. Dry the wok first by wiping the wok surface with paper towels (the paper towels may look gray after this). Then dry the wok thoroughly over the stovetop using low heat.
2 Open the pores of the wok by heating up all sides as well as the handles. Switch off the heat. Next, put vegetable oil (I use canola in a clear, plastic squeeze bottle) onto a couple of folded paper towels and apply a THIN, even coat to the inside and outside of the wok including the handles. Swish the oil around the wok in a quick motion. Turn the wok upside down on top of a sheet of foil and bake in the oven for 40 minutes. After the 40 minutes are up, leave the wok

in the oven to cool for about an hour. The wok should be cool to the touch prior to next step. If there's too much gray when you touch the wok, repeat steps 2 and 3 to ensure your seasoning is correct. *Note*: Do NOT pour the oil directly into wok or use too much oil, otherwise the oil will bake in sticky globs.
3 Wash the wok out with hot water and a green scrubber and no soap. Dry completely by using the stovetop over low heat. We are now ready to season the inside of the wok. First, chop an onion or a bunch of green onions (scallions) or chives, garlic, or ginger or some combination of these. This last step will help to finish the seasoning with an aromatic fragrance.
4 Do the following steps in quick sequence. Using oven pads:
5 Heat the wok on high heat till you see first wisps of smoke.
6 Immediately squeeze vegetable oil around the sides of the wok, go around 3–4

times so oil drips down sides.
7 Add the aromatics. Use a spatula to push the aromatics up the sides of the wok. You will see the seasoning (bronze color) start immediately.
8 Tip the wok back and forth so all the sides will get some heat.
9 Keep stir-frying until the seasoning (bronze) happens all around the wok, then toss the contents out. Your wok is now ready for your inaugural stir-fry!

Care and Maintenance of Your Wok

After using your wok, soak it in hot water (no soap) while you are eating but never for very long because it will begin to rust. Any food particles will lift off easily. Use a sink brush or green scrubber pad to remove any particles. Dry the wok by heating it over the stovetop over low heat. I do not wipe oil on my wok prior to storing because it can become rancid and sticky.

If your wok is looking dry, rub oiled paper towels all around it to restore its finish. Use your wok for cooking everything, not just Asian stir-fry, and the patina will build back up quickly!

If you get a crust on your wok from caramelizing (sugar), scrub it off with a green scrubber. Rub oiled paper towels in the problem area and heat on the stove, this will "reseason" it.

Do NOT put your wok in the dishwasher. The washing agent is too strong and the patina will fade and it will ruin your wok.

Eleanor Hoh is a cooking teacher and has been a cast iron wok advocate and enthusiast for over 20 years.

Understanding Chinese Ingredients

It's easier than ever to stock a Chinese pantry. With the proliferation of the ethnic sections at local supermarkets, common Chinese ingredients are no longer difficult to find, especially when it comes to items like soy sauce, oyster sauce, and sesame oil. More exotic Chinese ingredients can be purchased online at various Chinese/Asian grocery websites (Resource Guide, page 140). If you live in a small city where there is a concentrated Asian population, it's very likely that you will find an Asian food store or market that carries a supply of Chinese ingredients. If you live by the coast or near a major city with a Chinatown, (for example: San Francisco, Los Angeles, New York, Washington DC, Chicago, Seattle, Portland, or Honolulu) consider yourself lucky because you can get just about any Chinese ingredient at the many markets there. If you are unsure about where to go, just ask your Asian or Chinese friends and I am almost certain that they will point you to a good source. Building a Chinese pantry is both fun and rewarding. Here is the list of the most common Chinese ingredients I use on a daily basis and are used in the recipes of this cookbook.

Bamboo Shoots are the edible young and tender stems of bamboo plants. Bamboo shoots are available either fresh or canned, but canned bamboo shoots are the most easily found and probably safest to use as some fresh bamboo shoots have a strong and unappetizing odor. Canned bamboo shoots are already cooked and come sliced, whole, or in thin strips. I prefer the sliced version so I can use it for stir-fries, and I can cut them into thin strips for Hot and Sour Soup (page 55).

Bok Choy is a common Chinese vegetable that has white stems with green leaves. Bok choy has a mild flavor and the white stems are always crisp. They come in different sizes but the one I love most is baby bok choy, which is about 3-4 inches (7-10 cm) in length. They are very versatile and can be used in stir-fries, soups, or to add texture and color to noodle dishes.

Chicken Bouillon Powder (Chicken Powder) is the secret ingredient used by many Chinese chefs and home cooks. It's a superior flavoring agent because it's made with real chicken. I love it as a marinade or as a seasoning. Chicken bouillon powder is also marketed as "chicken powder" or "chicken seasoning powder." I prefer Knorr brand, which has a no-MSG version.

Chinese Black Vinegar is made of fermented rice, wheat, barley, or sorghum and often labeled as "Chinkiang vinegar." It's used as a dipping sauce for dumplings. It's very dark in color with a mouth-puckering flavor. When it's used in cooking, it imparts a complex, tart, and smoky flavor to dishes.

Chinese Broccoli (*gailan/kailan*) is a dark green vegetable with thick stalks. The leaves are sturdier when compared to other Chinese greens, and resemble kale, and so it's sometimes called Chinese kale.

If you shop in a Chinese or Asian store, Chinese broccoli is often labeled as *gailan* or *kailan*.

Chinese Chives (Garlic Chives) This green, flat, and grass-like vegetable has a distinctly garlicky flavor, an ideal ingredient for Chinese dumplings or *jiaozi*. When shopping for Chinese chives, make sure that you don't confuse it with regular green onions (scallions), which have hollow leaves. Chinese chives are believed to have antiseptic qualities and so many people combine it with oil to season a new wok. **Yellow Chives** are basically Chinese chives (garlic chives) that have been grown in the dark, that is, without the exposure to sunlight. As a result, yellow chives are stripped of the green color found in regular Chinese chives.

Yellow chives are commonly used in Cantonese cuisine, such as soups and noodles. They are best used when fresh because they don't keep well in the refrig-

Yellow Garlic Chives

Garlic Chives

Chinese Broccoli

Bok Choy

Dried Shiitake Mushroom

Wood Ear Mushroom

Bamboo Shoot Strips

Water Chestnuts

Sliced Bamboo Shoots

erator. If they become stale they will emit a strong and unpleasant smell.

Chinese Rice Vinegar is clear in color, has a sharp and acidic smell, and has a tart taste. It's used to pickle vegetables as well as to give a sour taste to some Chinese dishes. Chinese rice vinegar is usually sold in a tall glass bottle. A bottle will last forever because it's used sparingly in recipes. It keeps well at room temperature or in the refrigerator.

Chinese Rice Wine is used in many recipes in this book. I prefer Shaoxing wine, which is an amber-hued wine produced in the town of Shaoxing, in the Zhejiang province of China. It has a low alcohol content and is great for marinating proteins. When added to sauces, it imparts a hint of alcohol flavoring. Dry sherry is a great substitute for Chinese rice wine.

Chinese Rose Wine This intense and highly aromatic wine is called *Mei Kuei Lu Chiew* in Chinese. It's sometimes labeled as Rose Essence Wine in English. Chinese rose wine is basically sorghum liquor that is distilled with rock sugar and rose petals, and is about 46% alcohol! Hailed as the Chinese brandy, it's used in marinating meats such as BBQ pork or *char siu*. Because of its strong alcohol flavor, it's used sparingly but infuses the marinated meats with an unforgettable aroma.

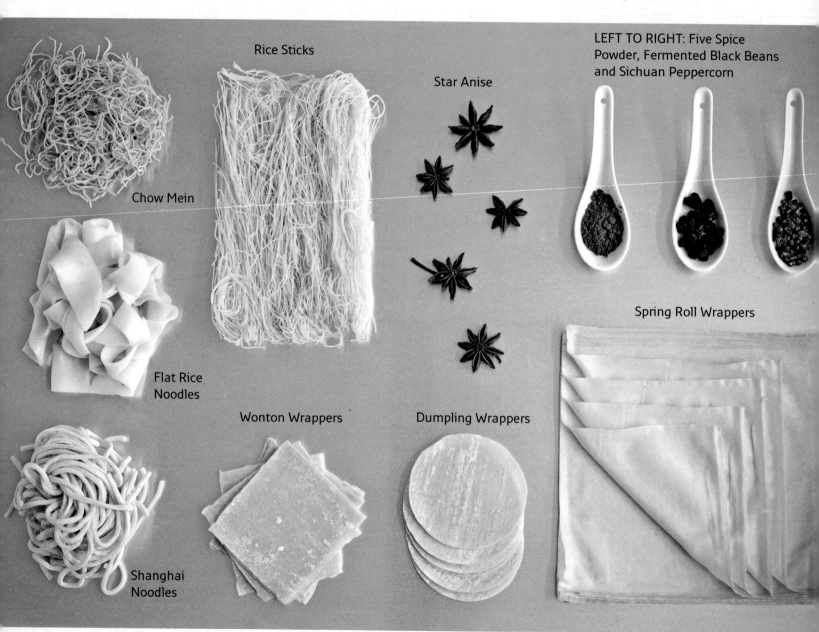

Rice Sticks

Star Anise

LEFT TO RIGHT: Five Spice Powder, Fermented Black Beans and Sichuan Peppercorn

Chow Mein

Spring Roll Wrappers

Flat Rice Noodles

Wonton Wrappers

Dumpling Wrappers

Shanghai Noodles

Dried Shiitake Mushrooms are readily available in Chinese markets. They are reconstituted in water before using. Dried shiitake mushrooms have a wonderful "umami" flavor that makes it a great addition to a variety of dishes, from soups to dim sum and dumplings. Dried shiitake mushrooms keep in the pantry or refrigerator for a long time, but make sure they are stored in a sealed container or plastic bag so they don't lose their smoky aroma.

Fermented Black Beans Pungent and salty, fermented black beans are the basic ingredient of Chinese black bean sauce. They are usually available in a plastic or paper packet, and labeled as "fermented black beans," "preserved black beans," or "salted black beans." Before using, they must be rinsed and soaked in cold water.

Fish Sauce While fish sauce is an essential part of Vietnamese and Thai cuisines, it's not an uncommon ingredient in Chinese cooking, especially in Southern Chinese cooking from Fujian and Chaozhou. Fish sauce is pungent, but a little dash adds a new taste dimension to many dishes.

Five Spice Powder is a blend of five spices: star anise, Sichuan peppercorn, cloves, cassia or cinnamon, and fennel seeds (although white pepper, licorice, and ginger might be used in other variations). Chinese five spice powder has an exotic aroma and it's highly concentrated. It's mostly used to marinate pork or poultry because it imparts a complex taste and a striking smell to roasted meat. It's also used to flavor the stewing stock for Chinese Tea Leaf Eggs (page 107).

Hoisin Sauce This sweet and savory sauce is an essential ingredient for many Chinese recipes. It can be used as a dipping sauce, marinade, or a flavoring sauce in Chinese stir-fries. The complex flavor of hoisin sauce comes from the fermented soybeans, spices, dried sweet potatoes, salt, sugar, and other ingredients.

Hot Bean Sauce (*Dou Ban Jiang*) Hot Bean Sauce is used in Sichuan cuisine as a flavoring paste. It's made with salted soybeans and chilies. In Chinese, it's called *dou ban jiang* and it can be labeled as "hot bean paste," "chili bean paste," or "chili bean sauce." Hot bean sauce is usually sold in small glass jars.

Maltose also known as malt sugar, is a sticky and sweet syrup made from malt. Maltose is the secret ingredient used in Chinese BBQ or roasted meats, such as Cantonese BBQ Pork (page 81) and Peking duck. I recommend MapleWood Maltose, a product of China. Maltose keeps well in the refrigerator, but once chilled, it becomes extremely gummy and almost rock solid. Leave it out at room temperature for a few hours before attempting to extract it from the container.

Noodles There are many types of noodles used in Chinese cooking: fresh, dried, and of different shapes and forms. Here are some of the most-loved Chinese noodles that I use regularly for delicious noodle dishes. **Chow Mein** The best chow mein is fresh chow mein, and these are available in a clear plastic packet at Chinese or Asian markets. There are two types of fresh chow mein: steamed chow mein or pan-fried chow mein. For regular Homestyle Chow Mein Noodles (page 126), I prefer steamed chow mein, which is softer in texture. For Crispy Pan-fried Noodles (page 129), I use pan-fried chow mein, which is dryer and makes for easier pan-frying. If you can't find fresh chow mein where you are, you can always use dried chow mein or egg noodles for the recipes in this cookbook. **Flat Rice Noodles** Flat rice noodles are available fresh at Chinese or Asian stores. They are white in color, coated with oil, soft, and pliable. They keep for a good 3-4 days in the refrigerator, but once refrigerated, they will need to be warmed to room temperature before using. Flat rice noodles are usually cut ¾ inch (2 cm) wide but they also come in uncut sheets. For the recipes in this cookbook, get the pre-cut flat rice noodles. **Rice Sticks** (Rice Vermicelli) Rice sticks or rice vermicelli are dry, thin, rice noodles made with rice flour and water. They are mostly imported from China, even though there are brands from Taiwan, which are thinner. In the United States they are often labeled as rice sticks, and some brands label it as rice vermicelli or vermicelli. When shopping for rice sticks, check the label to make sure that no starch was added. I dislike those made with starch—they tend to stick to the bottom of the wok and clump together during the cooking process. **Shanghai Noodles** Shanghai noodles are a variety of fresh noodles that are thicker and chewier than other noodles. It's usually packaged in a clear plastic bag and labeled as thick noodles, plain thick noodles, or Shanghai noodles. They are available at Asian supermarkets or Chinese delis. If you can't find this variety of noodle, you can use any noodle that is broader than regular egg noodles. If you like, you can even use udon.

Oyster Sauce Other than soy sauce, oyster sauce is another essential flavoring sauce in Chinese cooking. Made from oyster extract, oyster sauce is dark brown or caramel in color. Its salty, rich oyster flavor is used in many Chinese stir-fries. Please take note that MSG (Monosodium Glutamate) might be added to an oyster sauce as a flavor enhancer, so read the label carefully to find the one that best suits your eating habits.

Plum Sauce is made of salted plum, rice vinegar, salt, sugar, and water. It's a wonderful flavoring sauce that is both sweet and sour. I use plum sauce to make Chinese sweet-and-sour dishes because it enhances and balances the overall taste of the final product.

Rock Sugar can be found in either yellow or white crystals, but I prefer the yellow variety. The taste is sweet yet subtle and I use it to make the Cantonese-Style Steamed Fish Sauce (page 28), which imparts a deeper flavor than regular sugar. Rock sugar keeps forever in the pantry or refrigerator. If you live in a damp and humid place, store rock sugar in the refrigerator.

Sichuan Peppercorn is a vital ingredient in Sichuan cuisine. It doesn't taste hot like white or black pepper and it's mostly used for its unique lemony aroma, exotic flavor, and the tingly numbing sensation it gives the mouth. When combined with chili, the duo delivers the *mala* flavor, which is the key characteristic of Sichuan cooking.

Sesame Oil is made from pressed and toasted sesame seeds, and it's a very popular ingredient in Chinese cooking. The strong sesame taste and nutty fragrance makes it a great marinade for meats and seafood. It's used primarily as flavoring oil and not as a cooking oil. When shopping for sesame oil, look for the dark-amber 100% pure sesame oil to achieve the best results.

Soy Sauce I can't think of a Chinese pantry without soy sauce—a condiment made of fermented soybeans, salt, and water. There are many types of soy sauce in the market: light soy sauce, low-sodium soy sauce, superior soy sauce, mushroom-flavored soy sauce, and the list goes on.

For the recipes in this book, I use a regular soy sauce. I recommend getting soy sauce that's made in Taiwan or Hong Kong.
Dark Soy Sauce As its name suggests, this is a darker, blacker, and thicker variety than regular soy sauce. Please take note that dark soy sauce is used for adding color to the food and not so much for its taste, so use it sparingly.

Star Anise is an 8-point star shape seed or fruit of the star anise tree. Star anise is an important spice in Chinese cooking. It's one of the major ingredients used in Chinese five spice powder and used to infuse the Tea Leaf Eggs (page 107) in this cookbook.

Sweet Bean Sauce There are many types of sweet bean sauce, but the most common ones are made of fermented soybean paste with sugar, thickened with flour. It's the essential flavoring sauce for Sichuan Twice-Cooked Pork (page 77). Sweet bean sauce can be found at Asian supermarkets or online stores. If you can't find it, you can replace it with hoisin sauce.

White Pepper comes from the peppercorn plant. In Chinese cooking, white pepper is definitely the preferred choice because of its milder taste. White pepper is available in both powder form and whole peppercorns. For Chinese cooking, the former is mostly used to flavor sauces, soups, or as a table condiment or marinade.

Water Chestnuts are aquatic plants that grow in marshes. It's an important ingredient in Chinese cuisine because it adds a sweet taste and lends a nice crunch to the final product. Fresh water chestnuts are available in Chinese or Asian supermarkets, but canned water chestnuts can be found at regular food stores.

Wood Ear Mushroom refers to a tree ear fungus. It's sometimes marketed as wood ear mushroom, or black fungus. Wood ear has a very mild flavor; it's mostly revered for its crunchy texture, making it excellent for hot and sour soup, *siu mai*, water dumplings, and some stir-fry dishes.

Maltose

Sesame Oil

Chicken Bouillon Powder

Hot Bean Sauce

Sweet Bean Sauce

Wood ears are always sold dried in packages, and need to be reconstituted with hot water before using. Commercially, they are available whole or shredded. I always get the whole ones because they can be easily reconstituted with water and cut into thin strips or whatever the shape called for in the recipes.

Spring Roll Wrappers Spring roll wrappers can be found in the frozen section of Chinese or Asian markets. They usually come in two sizes: 4-inch or 8-inch squares. I prefer the latter because they are easier to handle. Please take note that the best spring roll wrappers should be very thin. I don't recommend egg roll wrappers, which are pale yellow in color and much thicker. Egg roll wrappers are used to make the American-version of egg rolls and not the traditional crispy Chinese spring rolls.

Wrappers There are a variety of dumpling wrappers available at the market: wonton, pot stickers, *siu mai, jiaozi, gyoza*, etc., and it can be overwhelming if you are not familiar with them. Don't be confused by the name—they are actually quite similar except that wonton wrappers are usually yellow in color because of the addition of egg (or artificial coloring) in the ingredients. Here are my simple pointers when shopping for dumpling wrappers:

1 Pot stickers, *jiaozi*, and *gyoza* wrappers are pretty much the same product. They are usually round.

2 Wonton wrappers and *siu mai* wrappers are similar to each other. They are pale yellow or yellow in color and usually come in squares.

3 For Pork Dumpling Soup (page 52), if you can find *Siu Kow* (Water Dumplings) wrappers in your store, use them, but if not, wonton wrappers will work just fine.

The Basics

This is a collection of basic recipes that will make this cookbook more accessible for you. This is by no means the most comprehensive list of basics for Chinese cooking, but sauces such as Sweet-and-Sour Sauce (page 30), Chinese Barbeque Sauce (page 29), Cantonese-Style Steamed Fish Sauce (page 28) are very versatile because they can be easily adapted to create vegetarian or vegan dishes. I have also included simple flavored oil recipes—Chili Oil (page 27) and Sichuan Peppercorn Oil (page 27)—two wonderful infused oils for authentic Sichuan dishes. Condiments and dipping sauces such as the Pickled Green Chilies (page 28) and the Dumpling Dipping Sauce (page 71) complement freshly made dumplings and noodle dishes beautifully!

Steamed Rice Mi fan

Steamed rice is the foundation of Chinese cooking—it is the staple of almost every Chinese meal. The Chinese words *chi fan*, which literally means: "eat rice" are probably two of the most beloved words in the Chinese language. *Chi fan* evokes many happy visual images in my mind: when a father comes home after a hard day of work and greets his family over the dinner table; a hungry child eagerly shoveling a bowl of steaming hot rice to his mouth using a pair of chopsticks; fond memories with my late parents when I piled their favorite foods on top of their rice as they smiled contently at my loving gesture. You can't make Chinese food if you don't know how to prepare moist, soft, and fluffy steamed rice. Here is my steamed rice recipe for use with an electronic rice cooker or stovetop preparation.

Serves 4

2 cups (400 g) rice, long grain or jasmine rice
2 cups (500 ml) water

Using an Electronic Rice Cooker
1 Place the rice inside the cooking pan of an electronic rice cooker.
2 Rinse the rice with cold running water, swishing and stirring quickly by hand. When the water turns murky, drain the water immediately. Repeat the same for 3–4 times until the water becomes almost clear. Drain the excess water and leave 2 cups of water in the cooking pan.
3 Turn the heat on the rice cooker to boil the rice (according to your rice cooker's manual).
4 Stir and loosen the rice immediately with the rice spatula after cooking has completed.

Using the Stovetop
1 Place the rice inside a pot.
2 Rinse the rice with cold running water, swishing and stirring quickly by hand. When the water turns murky, drain the water immediately. Repeat 3–4 times until the water becomes almost clear. Drain the excess water and leave 2 cups of water in the pot.
3 Cover the pot with its lid and bring to a boil over medium heat on a stovetop. Boil for 15 minutes or until the rice is cooked and all the liquid has been absorbed by the rice.
4 Stir and loosen the rice immediately with the rice spatula or a pair of wooden chopsticks. Cover the pot and let rest for about 10 minutes before serving.

Chili Oil   La You

Chinese cuisine consists of many regional cooking styles, one of my favorites is Sichuan cuisine. Sichuan food is famous for its *ma* (numbing) and *la* (spicy) flavors. For the *la* flavor, dried red chilies are used abundantly, but chili oil also plays a key role in lending a spicy nuance to dishes.

Bottled chili oil (*la you*) is commonly found at Asian grocery stores, but I love making mine from scratch. I always make a small portion, just enough for cooking a few Sichuan dishes. I don't like the smell of stale oil, so the good news is that it is extremely simple to make my own so I can always have the freshest chili oil on hand.

Makes ⅓ cup (80 ml)

¼ cup (35 g) dried red pepper flakes
½ cup (125 ml) oil

1 Place the dried red pepper flakes in a small bowl.
2 Heat the oil in a wok or skillet over high heat until it reaches the smoking point. Different oils have different temperatures of smoking point. The oil is ready when you see a swirl of white smoke coming out from it.
3 Pour the oil into the red pepper flakes. Stir the Chili Oil immediately with a pair of wooden chopsticks to help the red pepper flakes release their heat, aroma, and flavor. Let it cool for at least 2 hours, allowing the flavor to develop.
4 Drain the Chili Oil with a fine strainer into a glass jar. Discard the strained pepper flakes. The oil is now ready for use.

Sichuan Peppercorn Oil   Hua Jiao You

Sichuan peppercorn is a distinct ingredient in Sichuan cuisine that provides the signature *ma* (numbing) flavor in the mouth. If you haven't tried real Sichuan food, the numbing sensation might be hard to imagine. I always explain it as the "tingly and crawly" feeling that numbs the lips and the inside of the mouth. I am personally addicted to the *ma* flavor, so I always have Sichuan Peppercorn Oil in my kitchen. Both Chili Oil and Sichuan peppercorn oil are used to prepare two of my favorite Sichuan dishes: Sichuan Spicy Chicken (page 89) and Mapo Tofu (page 109).

Makes ⅓ cup (80 ml)

¼ cup (10 g) Sichuan peppercorns
½ cup (125 ml) oil

1 Place the Sichuan peppercorns in a small bowl.
2 Heat the oil in a wok or skillet over high heat until it reaches the smoking point. Different oils have different temperatures of smoking point. The oil is ready when you see a swirl of white smoke coming out from it.
3 Add the oil into the Sichuan peppercorns. Stir the Sichuan Peppercorn Oil immediately with a pair of wooden chopsticks to help the Sichuan peppercorns release their aroma and flavor. Let it cool for at least 2 hours to develop the flavor.
4 Drain the Sichuan Peppercorn Oil into a glass jar using a fine strainer. Discard the peppercorns. The oil is now ready for use.

Pickled Green Chilies

If you have dined at Cantonese noodle restaurants, I am sure you have seen Pickled Green Chilies in one of the condiment canisters. The Chinese love Pickled Green Chilies as a condiment for noodles. It is usually mixed in a saucer with a little soy sauce and eaten with the noodles.

The acidity and the moderate heat of Pickled Green Chilies perks up the taste of many Cantonese-style noodle dishes, such as Crispy Pan-fried Noodles (page 129), Beef Chow Fun Noodles (page 123), or Seafood Chow Fun Noodles (page 122). Pickled Green Chilies also keeps well in the refrigerator, for up to two weeks. While handling the green chilies, it's best to wear gloves, or just make sure that you don't rub your eyes afterwards!

Makes approximately 1½ cups

4 oz (100 g) green finger-length chilies
1 cup (250 ml) water
1 cup (250 ml) Chinese rice vinegar
1 teaspoon salt
½ teaspoon sugar

> **COOK'S NOTE:** If you are in the United States, I recommend using green Serrano or Jalapeño chilies.
> Do not touch your eyes or face after handling the green chilies.

1 Cut the green chilies into rings and rinse with cold running water. Place the chilies in a bowl.
2 Bring the water to a boil and pour it over the chilies. Let the chilies sit in the boiled water, about 10 seconds. Drain and discard the water.
3 Add the vinegar, salt, and sugar into the chilies. Stir to blend well.
4 Transfer everything into a small glass container or canister jar and leave it in the refrigerator. The pickled green chilies will be ready the next day.

Cantonese-style Steamed Fish Sauce

For seafood such as fish and oyster, the Chinese, especially the Cantonese, revere simple steaming while using the most basic of ingredients: ginger, green onions (scallions), and a light soy sauce dressing that accentuates the natural flavors of the seafood. If you have a great soy sauce dressing, you are almost guaranteed to have a successful dish, whether you are making steamed fish, oyster, or even shrimp.

It is very important that you use a high-quality soy sauce when making this Cantonese-style Steamed Fish Sauce. For that, I recommend finding a soy sauce made in Hong Kong or Taiwan.

Makes ½ cup (125 ml) or for 1½ to 2 lbs (750 g to 1 kg) fish or 8 big oysters on the half shell

3 tablespoons soy sauce
1 tablespoon Chinese rice wine or sherry
2 tablespoons water
¼ teaspoon sesame oil
3 dashes white pepper
2 tablespoons rock sugar
1 tablespoon oil

1 Mix all the ingredients in a small bowl and set aside.
2 Heat a saucepan over medium to low heat. Stir in the sauce to blend well.
3 Once the sauce starts to bubble and boil, remove the saucepan from the heat and let it cool.

> **COOK'S NOTE:** Rock sugar usually comes in small to medium-sized solid blocks. For easy measurement, break and grind the rock sugar into a powder form using a mortar and pestle.

Chinese BBQ Sauce   Cha Shao Jiang

My good friend, Shirley Lim, came up with this savory, rich, and absolutely addictive Chinese BBQ Sauce, with the perfect ratio of the four key ingredients: maltose, honey, hoisin sauce, and soy sauce. Chinese rose wine is another secret ingredient used in this recipe. The higher alcohol content and distilled rose petals in the rose wine deliver an incredible dimension of flavor to the sauce. Once you try this sauce, you will probably never go back to the bottled instant char siu sauce.

This sauce is highly versatile and used in many recipes in this cookbook: Cantonese BBQ Pork (page 81), Baked BBQ Pork Puffs (page 63), and Tangy BBQ Pork Ribs (page 44). It also pairs well with chicken and is great as a stir-fry sauce.

Makes ½ cup (125 ml)

1½ tablespoons maltose
1½ tablespoons honey
1½ tablespoons hoisin sauce
1½ tablespoons soy sauce
1 teaspoon Chinese rose wine, rice wine, or sherry
3 dashes white pepper
½ teaspoon Chinese five spice powder
½ teaspoon sesame oil

1 Mix all the ingredients in a small bowl and set aside.
2 Heat a saucepan over medium to low heat. Stir in the sauce and blend well.
3 Once the sauce starts to bubble and boil, remove the saucepan from the heat and let it cool.

> **COOK'S NOTE:** If you can't find maltose, double up on the portion of honey.

Shrimp Mousse   Xia Jiang

Shrimp Mousse is a common stuffing widely used in Chinese cuisine, especially in dim sum and appetizers. Shrimp mousse is easy to prepare at home and is used for many recipes in this book: Sesame Shrimp Toasts (page 39), Stuffed Crab Claws (page 40), Crunchy Shrimp Balls (page 42), and Crispy Shrimp Dumplings (page 60). A great Shrimp Mousse relies on the freshness of the shrimp, so find the freshest shrimp possible to ensure the best texture. Other than dim sum and appetizers, you can also use Shrimp Mousse as a filling for tofu or for vegetables like eggplant and okra.

Makes 8 oz (250 g)

8 oz (250 g) shelled and deveined raw shrimp

Seasonings
1 tablespoon egg white
3 dashes white pepper
½ teaspoon salt
½ teaspoon sugar
¼ teaspoon sesame oil
½ tablespoon oil
½ tablespoon cornstarch

1 Rinse the shrimp with cold running water. Pat dry with paper towels.
2 Add the shrimp and all the ingredients in the Seasonings to a food processor.
3 Turn on the food processor to blend well, or until the shrimp mixture becomes sticky and cohesive.
4 Alternatively, you can pound and mince the Shrimp Mousse with a Chinese cleaver as shown below.

Sweet-and-Sour Sauce

I had to experiment several times to get this Sweet-and-Sour Sauce perfect. It tastes nothing like the starch-laden and sickly sweet version you get in most Chinese restaurants in the United States.

I jazzed up my Sweet-and-Sour Sauce with two special ingredients: plum sauce and Lea & Perrins Worcestershire sauce. They imbue the Sweet-and-Sour Pork (page 80) and Sweet-and-Sour Fish (page 102) with a deeper, rounder, and more intense taste structure. If you don't eat meat or seafood, you can easily use vegetarian and vegan-friendly ingredients to make your own version of sweet-and-sour dishes. You can even make it into a dipping sauce, which goes well with fried tofu, chicken, or fish nuggets.

Makes ½ cup (125 ml)

2 tablespoons ketchup
1 tablespoon plum sauce
½ tablespoon Worcestershire sauce
1 teaspoon Chinese rice vinegar
½ tablespoon oyster sauce
1 teaspoon sugar
4 tablespoons water
¼ teaspoon sesame oil
1 teaspoon cornstarch

1 Mix all the ingredients in a small bowl and then use it as instructed in the recipe.
2 If you are making it into a dipping sauce, heat a saucepan over medium heat. Transfer the Sweet-and-Sour Sauce into the saucepan and stir to blend well.
3 Turn off the heat as soon as the sauce starts to bubble. Remove the saucepan from the heat and let it cool.

Cucumber Salad

There is a general misconception that Chinese food is unhealthy, greasy, and mostly deep-fried. In reality, there are many fresh and healthy Chinese recipes, such as this refreshing and crisp Cucumber Salad. Chinese salad is often served as a cold appetizer during a multicourse meal with the intention of cleaning one's palate and preparing one's appetite for the main courses.

This Cucumber Salad is really simple to prepare. Make it ahead of time to allow the vinegar to treat the cucumber and make it crunchy.

Serves 4 as an appetizer as part of multicourse meal

1 cucumber, about 8 oz (250 g)
1 teaspoon salt
2 teaspoons sugar
2 teaspoons Chinese rice vinegar

1 Rinse the cucumber thoroughly with cold running water.
2 Quarter the cucumber lengthwise. Remove and discard the seeds. Slice the cucumber diagonally into pieces, each about ¹/₃-inch (1 cm) thick.
3 Transfer the sliced cucumber into a bowl, add the salt and mix well. Set aside for 30 minutes.
4 Drain the water and add the sugar and Chinese rice vinegar to the cucumber. Stir to blend well. Chill in the refrigerator for at least an hour before serving.

Homemade Chicken Stock

When it comes to Homemade Chicken Stock, I am a firm believer that less is more—all you really need is a stewing chicken (stewing hen), which is superior for making chicken stock, some ginger, and water. If you can't find stewing chicken, regular chicken will work nearly as well.

Even though I prefer Homemade Chicken Stock, I also use canned chicken broth in my Chinese cooking. It's a convenient substitute and delivers satisfactory results.

Makes 6 cups (1.5 liters)

1 whole stewing chicken (stewing hen) or regular chicken, about 2 lbs (1 kg)
10 cups (2.25 liters) water
One 2 in (5 cm) piece fresh ginger, peeled and smashed
2 teaspoons salt

1 Cut the chicken into pieces. Remove all the skin, except on the wings. Cut out all the excess fat and rinse the chicken under cold running water.
2 Bring the water to a boil in a stockpot. Add the chicken, ginger, and salt. Boil over high heat for 20 minutes. Skim the surface.
3 Cover the pot and turn the heat to low. Simmer the chicken broth for 4 hours. Turn off the heat and let it cool.
4 Drain the chicken stock with a strainer. Discard the chicken and ginger. The chicken stock can be used right away or it can be refrigerated for up to one month.

Homemade Dumpling Wrappers

This is a basic dumpling wrapper recipe for Delicious Pot Stickers (page 66), Pork and Chive Dumplings (page 68), Steamed Chicken and Mushroom Dumplings (Page 69), and Shrimp with Yellow Chive Dumplings (page 70). For these recipes, store-bought dumpling wrappers are probably the most convenient. However, if you are in the mood to prepare everything from scratch, you can make your own Dumpling Wrapper and it takes only two ingredients.

Makes 20

1 cup (130 g) all-purpose flour
¼ cup (65 ml) water plus 1 teaspoon water
Some additional all-purpose flour, for dusting and rolling

How to Make the Dumpling Wrappers
1 Combine the all-purpose flour and water in a container to form the dough. Knead the dough until it is no longer sticky and the surface becomes smooth, about 10–15 minutes. Cover the dough with a damp cloth and let it rest for 30 minutes.
2 On a flat and floured surface, divide the dough into two equal portions and roll them into cylinders, 1 inch (2.5 cm) in diameter and 5 inches (12.75 cm) in length.
3 Cut each cylinder into 10 equal pieces, each about ¹/₂-inch (1.25 cm) thick.
4 Dust the rolling pin with some all-purpose flour and roll the dough until flat, measuring about 3¹/₂ inches (9 cm) in diameter. To make the wrapper round in shape, use a 3 ½ -inch (9 cm) cookie cutter to trim off the uneven edges.

Chapter 1

Appetizers

I am big on appetizers, and I am especially partial to Chinese appetizers. What's not to love about these little munchies? Great tasting treats like refreshing Tasty Lettuce Wraps (page 34), Salt and Pepper Squid (page 35), Crispy Fried Wontons (page 36), and aromatic Green Onion Pancakes (page 46) are wonderful.

In China, appetizers are mostly served as cold dishes (called *leng cai* or *liang cai*): smoked meats, cured offal, and pickled vegetables. In this chapter, I have included all the popular hot appetizers to suit your palate. These appetizers are commonly found in Chinese restaurants in the United States, and now you can make them in the comfort of your own home. Enjoy!

Tasty Lettuce Wraps

As much as I wanted to believe that the Lettuce Wrap is a PF Chang's invention, I would be wrong. Lettuce Wrap is indeed a Chinese recipe but it's the PF Chang Empire that makes it one of the most popular and recognizable appetizers in the United States.

There is nothing not to like about Lettuce Wraps—they taste great, they're refreshing, and it's always fun to play with your food. Wrapping the filling in the lettuce leaf is half the fun, and popping the crisp and cold Lettuce Wrap filled with goodies into your mouth is itself a commodity that launched the billion-dollar empire of PF Chang.

Serves 4 as an appetizer

3 dried shiitake mushrooms
8 oz (250 g) skinless, boneless chicken thighs, ground
3 fresh water chestnuts, chopped finely
2 tablespoons oil
2 cloves garlic, minced
1 head iceberg lettuce, rinsed
1 heaping tablespoon chopped green onion (scallion)

Seasonings
1 tablespoon soy sauce
½ teaspoon oyster sauce
¼ teaspoon dark soy sauce
½ teaspoon sesame oil
1 tablespoon Chinese rice wine or sherry
½ teaspoon sugar
3 dashes white pepper

Spicy Hoisin Dipping Sauce
4 tablespoons hoisin sauce
½ teaspoon chili sauce or to taste
1 tablespoon warm water

1 Soak the dried shiitake mushrooms in warm water in a small bowl until they become soft. Squeeze the mushrooms dry with your hand, discard the stems, cut and dice the mushroom caps into tiny pieces.

2 Combine the ground chicken meat, mushrooms and water chestnuts with all the Seasonings ingredients. Marinate for 15 minutes.

3 Mix all the Spicy Hoisin Dipping Sauce ingredients in a small saucer or bowl. Set aside.

4 Heat the oil in a wok or skillet over high heat. Add the garlic and then stir-fry to light brown before adding the ground chicken.

5 Using the spatula, stir the chicken continuously to loosen and break up the lumps. Continue to stir-fry until the chicken is cooked. Dish out and set aside.

6 Peel off each lettuce leaf from the iceberg lettuce carefully. Do not break the leaves.

7 Scoop two heaping tablespoons of the chicken and place it in the middle of a lettuce leaf. Wrap it up and dip the lettuce wrap into the Spicy Hoisin Dipping Sauce before eating. Garnish with green onion (scallion).

Salt and Pepper Squid

Salt and pepper, these most basic ingredients in the kitchen perform wonders for Chinese deep-fried dishes, such as this Salt and Pepper Squid. This popular dish can be made at home without much hassle, especially with the pre-cleaned squid tubes that you can find at the seafood sections of many supermarkets. My recipe calls for a two-step process that promises restaurant-style Salt and Pepper Squid. First, deep-fry the squid with a light and crispy frying batter, and then lightly toss the fried squid in a wok with chopped green onion, red chili, salt, and pepper. The end result is a serving of Salt and Pepper Squid that tastes like it's straight from a Chinese restaurant kitchen!

Serves 4 as an appetizer

10 oz (330 g) cleaned squid tubes, cut into
  1½ in (3.75 cm) width x 3 in (7.5 cm) length
¾ teaspoon salt
¾ teaspoon white pepper
Oil, for deep-frying
½ tablespoon oil, for stir-frying
1 heaping tablespoon chopped green onion
  (scallion)
1 teaspoon chopped red finger-length chili

Frying Batter
½ cup (65 g) all-purpose flour
¼ cup (35 g) cornstarch
½ teaspoon baking soda
1 egg white
½ cup (125 ml) water
1 tablespoon oil
A pinch of salt

1 Rinse the squid with cold running water. Pat dry with paper towels and then marinate with the 1/4 teaspoon of salt and 1/4 teaspoon of white pepper, about 15 minutes.
2 Mix all the ingredients for the Frying Batter until well combined. Add the squid to the Frying Batter, stir to coat evenly.
3 To deep-fry the squid, heat 2 to 3 inches (5 to 7.5 cm) of the oil in a wok or stockpot to 350°F (175°C). Gently drop the squid into the oil and loosen them up immediately with the spatula to prevent the squid from clumping together.
4 Deep-fry the squid to a light golden brown or until the batter becomes crispy. Do not overcook the squid or they will become tough and rubbery. Dish out with a strainer or slotted spoon, draining the excess oil by laying the squid on a wire rack or a dish lined with paper towels.
5 To stir-fry, heat the 1/2 tablespoon of oil in a skillet over high heat. Add the chopped green onion and red chili and stir quickly for a few times. Return the fried squid to the skillet and then add the remaining salt and white pepper. Stir to combine all the ingredients well, dish out and serve immediately.

Crispy Fried Wontons

In the United States, at many Chinese restaurants, fried wontons are basically fried wonton wrappers cut into strips with no filling. Traditionally, however, wontons have a filling composed mostly of ground pork that is wrapped in a dough skin (wonton wrapper). Fried wonton is a great finger food that I love to serve at gatherings and parties because everyone enjoys these deep-fried and glorious golden brown parcels of goodness. They are very easy to make and you can be creative with the filling. The base in this recipe is ground pork, but you can use chicken or even turkey. I love adding some shrimp to give it a richer and savorier taste, but I've had equal success using scallops and crabmeat.

Makes 24–36 or serves 6 as an
   appetizer or snack

**1 packet store-bought wonton
   wrappers**
Oil, for deep-frying

Filling
8 oz (250 g) ground pork
**4 oz (100 g) raw shrimp, finely
   chopped**
**One ½ in (1.25 cm) piece fresh
   ginger, peeled and grated**
**1 green onion (scallion),
   trimmed and cut into small
   rounds**
1 teaspoon sesame oil
**1 teaspoon Chinese rice wine
   or sherry**
1 teaspoon salt
3 dashes white pepper

1 Make the Filling by combining all the ingredients together. Chill the Filling in the refrigerator for 30 minutes.

2 Wrap the wontons by following the instructional picture guide on this page.

3 Heat 2 to 3 inches (5 to 7.5 cm) of the oil in a wok or stockpot to 350°F (175°C) for deep-frying. Gently drop the wrapped wontons into the oil and deep-fry in batches.

4 Deep-fry the wontons until they turn a light golden brown. Dish out with a strainer or slotted spoon, draining the excess oil by laying the wontons on a wire rack or a dish lined with paper towels. Serve immediately.

> **COOK'S NOTE:** There are different sizes of wonton wrappers in the marketplace. Use 1 teaspoon of the Filling if the wonton wrappers are smaller, which yields about 36 wontons.

HOW TO WRAP THE WONTONS

1 Place a piece of wonton wrapper on a flat surface and spoon about 1 tablespoon of the Filling onto the wrapper.

2 Make a circle with your left thumb and index finger. Place the wonton into the circle.

3 Fold the wonton by squeezing the opening tightly with your thumb and index finger.

4 Make sure the wrapped wonton is sealed tight and there is no leakage.

Sesame Shrimp Toasts

My earliest memory of Sesame Shrimp Toasts is a birthday party my family threw for me. Pieces of uniformly cut white toast (sans the crust) were filled with Shrimp Mousse (page 29), sprinkled with sesame seeds and then they were deep-fried to a glorious golden brown. The shrimp toast was an instant hit at the party and everyone loved it. The best shrimp toast should be crispy, airy, and light. It shouldn't be greasy and soaked in oil. For the best result, get a good quality white toast that is thicker and denser in texture (these don't absorb that much of the oil during the deep-frying process). Also, dropping the shrimp toast face down into the wok while frying certainly helps.

Makes 18 or serves 4 as an appetizer or snack

½ tablespoon chopped fresh coriander leaves
   (cilantro) or green onion (scallion)
1 recipe Shrimp Mousse (page 29)
3 pieces white bread toast
Oil, for deep-frying

Coating
3 tablespoons white sesame seeds
1 tablespoon black sesame seeds

1 Add the coriander leaves or green onion to the Shrimp Mousse and mix well. Set aside.

2 Cut off the crust of the white toast using a sharp knife. Discard the crusts and use only the white part of the toast. Cut each toast lengthwise into half, and then crosswise into six equal rectangle-shaped pieces.

3 Mix the Coating ingredients in a small plate and set aside.

4 Assemble the Sesame Shrimp Toasts by following the instructional picture guide below.

5 Heat 2 to 3 inches (5 to 7.5 cm) of the oil in a wok or stockpot to 350°F (175°C) for deep-frying. Gently drop the Sesame Shrimp Toasts into the oil and deep fry in batches.

6 Deep-fry until they turn light golden brown. Dish out with a strainer or slotted spoon, draining the excess oil by laying the Sesame Shrimp Toasts on a wire rack or a dish lined with paper towels. Serve immediately.

HOW TO MAKE THE SESAME SHRIMP TOASTS

1 Using a butterknife, spread about 1 tablespoon of the filling evenly atop each piece of the toast.

2 Roll the filling on the Coating mixture so the surface is completely covered with the sesame seeds.

3 A perfect Sesame Shrimp Toast before deep-frying.

Stuffed Crab Claws

I can't even begin to tell you how much I love this appetizer that combines two of my favorite seafoods in one bite-sized package—succulent crab claw encased in springy shrimp mousse. Each bite explodes with the luscious flavors of the shrimp and crab, and then there's the crispness of the breadcrumbs. The thought of this taste and texture combination makes my mouth water.

If you're a beginner, the assembling part might be a little challenging, but once you have a hang of it, it becomes relatively easy. For the crab claws, I recommend using frozen blue crab claws or snow crab claws.

Makes 8 or serves 2 as an appetizer or snack

8 frozen and pre-cracked crab claws
1 recipe Shrimp Mousse (page 29)
1 large egg
1 cup (50 g) bread crumbs or Japanese panko
Oil, for deep-frying

1 Defrost the crab claws. If the crab claws become watery after defrosting, pat dry with paper towels.
2 Lightly beat the egg in a bowl. Add the breadcrumbs to a deep plate. Set both of them aside.
3 Assemble the Stuffed Crab Claws by following the instructional picture guide below.
4 Heat 2 to 3 inches (5 to 7.5 cm) of the oil in a wok or stockpot to 350°F (175°C) for deep-frying. Gently drop the Stuffed Crab Claws into the oil and deep-fry in batches.
5 Deep-fry until they turn light golden brown. Dish out with a strainer or slotted spoon, draining the excess oil by laying the Stuffed Crab Claws on a wire rack or a dish lined with paper towels. Serve immediately.

HOW TO MAKE THE STUFFED CRAB CLAWS

1 Dab a little water on your fingers and wrap about 2 tablespoons of the Shrimp Mousse around the crabmeat. Make sure the Shrimp Mousse encases the crabmeat firmly and completely, revealing only the pointy claws. Dab more water on your fingers (if needed) to smooth over the Shrimp Mousse.

2 Dip the Stuffed Crab Claw immediately into the egg mixture.

3 Roll it around on the breadcrumbs for an even coating. Shake off the excess breadcrumbs. Repeat for the remaining crab claws.

Crunchy Shrimp Balls

I first tried this version of Crunchy Shrimp Balls at Ton Kiang, one of my favorite Chinese restaurants in San Francisco when I lived there many years ago, When my order arrived, I was immediately drawn to its appearance—golden-hued shrimp balls blanketed with crispy, shredded spring roll skins. At first bite I was smitten and fell instantly in love with this dainty appetizer. The spring roll skins make every bite a brittle crunch and, once you sink your teeth into the middle, the sweetness of the shrimp prevails.

Makes 10 or serves 2 as an appetizer or snack

1 recipe Shrimp Mousse (page 29)
6 pieces store-bought spring roll wrapper, 8 in square (20 cm square) in size
Oil, for deep-frying

1 Separate each sheet of the spring roll wrapper by hand.
2 Make the Fried Shrimp Balls by following the instructional picture guide on the opposite page.
3 Heat 2 to 3 inches (5 to 7.5 cm) of the oil in a wok or stockpot to 350°F (175°C) for deep-frying. Gently drop the shrimp balls into the oil and deep-fry in batches.
4 Deep-fry until they turn golden brown. Dish out with a strainer or slotted spoon, draining the excess oil by laying the Crunchy Shrimp Balls on a wire rack or a dish lined with paper towels. Serve immediately.

HOW TO MAKE THE SHRIMP BALLS

1 Roll three sheets of the spring roll wrapper into a loose cylinder. Using a pair of scissors, cut the wrappers into thin strips, about ⅛ inch (3 mm) in width. Repeat the same for the remaining wrappers. Loosen the cut wrappers by hand and transfer them to a plate. Cover with a damp cloth to prevent drying.

2 Wet both palms with some water and gently roll about 1 heaping tablespoon of the Shrimp Mousse into a ball.

3 Place the shrimp ball on top of the cut wrappers and roll it around to coat evenly.

4 The shrimp ball should be completely covered with a layer of cut wrappers and will resemble a fuzzy ball. Repeat the same for the remaining Shrimp Mousse.

Tangy BBQ Pork Ribs

Much like its close cousins, Cantonese BBQ Pork (page 81) and Crispy Roast Pork (page 76), Tangy BBQ Pork Ribs is another popular item offered at Chinese delis or Cantonese barbeque restaurants. You will often see them hanging at the display window, with its sticky glaze dripping.

While barbeque pork ribs can be served as a main dish and eaten with rice, I much prefer them as an appetizer. Like most people, I love eating these juicy ribs using my fingers. For the ribs, you can use either spare ribs or baby back ribs. If I am serving this as an appetizer, then I always prefer the baby back ribs.

Serves 4 as an appetizer

2 cloves garlic, minced
2 lbs (1 kg) pork spare ribs or baby back ribs
½ cup (125 ml) Chinese BBQ Sauce (page 29)
1 tablespoon oil

1 Rub the minced garlic evenly on both sides of the pork ribs. Marinate the pork ribs with ²/₃ (about 80 ml) of the Chinese BBQ Sauce for 8 hours or overnight. Add the oil into the remaining Chinese BBQ Sauce. Stir well and keep in the refrigerator.

2 The next day, preheat the oven to 325°F (160°C). Wrap the pork ribs with two layers of aluminum foil, place the parcel in a roasting pan and slow roast for about 2–3 hours. Make sure the aluminum foil is wrapped tightly around the ribs to prevent the juice or drippings from seeping out.

3 Remove the ribs from the oven after roasting, unwrap the aluminum foil carefully. If you like, you can save the juice or drippings in a small bowl as a dipping sauce. Brush both sides of the pork ribs with the remaining Chinese BBQ Sauce.

4 Put the ribs back into the oven (surface unwrapped) and broil on high heat until they are slightly charred, about 3 minutes.

5 Remove the ribs from the oven, cut into individual riblets and serve immediately.

COOK'S NOTE: If you like your ribs "falling off the bones," roast them for 3 hours.

Fried Chicken Wings

When I was pursuing my Master's Degree in the Midwest United States, I felt deprived of quality Chinese food. In my college town there were only two Chinese restaurants, both served standard American-Chinese fare. Fortunately, one of them also served some very tasty Fried Chicken Wings, so I would order those whenever I craved decent Chinese food. As a poor student, I only wished that I had the recipe so I could make it myself. My wish finally came true when a friend who worked as a kitchen helper at the restaurant revealed their recipe to me. The simple marinade of ginger, garlic, soy sauce, and oyster sauce creates succulent chicken wings with a garlicky-gingery fragrance and taste.

Serves 4 as an appetizer

1 lb (500 g) chicken wings, middle section and/or drumette
Oil, for deep-frying

Marinade
One 3 in (7.5 cm) piece fresh ginger, peeled
3 cloves garlic, finely minced
2 tablespoons soy sauce
1 tablespoon oyster sauce
½ teaspoon freshly ground black pepper
½ teaspoon salt

Coating
¼ cup (35 g) all-purpose flour
¼ cup (35 g) cornstarch

1 Rinse the chicken wings with cold running water. Pat dry with paper towels.

2 Make the Marinade by grating the fresh ginger. Squeeze the ginger pulp using your fingers to extract the juice. Discard the pulp. Mixed the remaining Marinade ingredients together until well combined. Marinate the chicken wings in the Marinade overnight.

3 The next day, combine the Coating ingredients in a bowl. Dust the chicken wings evenly with the Coating, shaking off the excess.

4 Heat 2 to 3 inches (5 to 7.5 cm) of the oil in a wok or stockpot to 350°F (175°C) for deep-frying. Gently drop the chicken wings into the oil and deep-fry in batches.

5 Deep-fry the wings until they turn a light golden brown. Dish out with a strainer or slotted spoon, draining the excess oil by laying the chicken wings on a wire rack or a dish lined with paper towels. Serve immediately.

Green Onion Pancakes

My first experience with Green Onion Pancakes was when I visited Shanghai for the first time. One morning, I was feeling jetlagged so I headed down to the hotel's lobby for an early morning breakfast. The breakfast set menu was traditional Chinese fare: freshly made soy bean milk, *you tiao* (fried cruller), tea leaf egg, and Green Onion Pancake.

As soon as my order arrived, I got a whiff of the green onions. The Green Onion Pancakes were crispy yet doughy in the middle, each bite was mildly salty and then the oniony fragrance surfaced. I enjoyed the pancakes thoroughly, especially with a glass of warm soybean milk, on that sleep-deprived morning.

The best Green Onion Pancakes are made with lard, so feel free to use lard (instead of oil) if you like.

Makes 8 pieces or serves 4 as an appetizer

1½ cups (200 g) all-purpose flour
1¼ teaspoons salt
½ cup (125 ml) water
3 green onions (scallions), green parts only, trimmed and cut
   into small rounds, to yield about ⅓ cup
2 tablespoons oil
Some additional all-purpose flour, for dusting and rolling
Oil, for frying

1 Sift the all-purpose flour into a big bowl and then add the salt into the flour. Combine well and set aside.
2 Bring the water to a boil. Slowly add the water to the flour and knead the dough until it's no longer sticky and the surface becomes smooth, about 10 minutes. If the dough is too dry, add 1 tablespoon of water to the dough. Cover the dough with a damp cloth and let it rest for 30 minutes.
3 Add the green onion into the dough and combine well.
4 Make the Green Onion Pancake by following the instructional picture guide on page 47.
5 Add about ¼ inch (6 mm) of oil into a stir-fry pan or skillet over moderately high heat. Transfer a piece of the pancake into the pan or skillet. Shallow fry each side of the pancake to a light golden brown, about 1 minute. Flip the pancake over and shallow fry the other side. Add more oil, repeat the same for the remaining pancakes and serve immediately.

HOW TO MAKE THE GREEN ONION PANCAKES

1 On a flat and floured surface, divide the dough into 8 equal-sized pieces. Roll each piece of dough into a ball using your palm.

2 Working with one dough ball at a time, roll the dough to a thin disc using a rolling pin. Dust the rolling pin with some all-purpose flour as you go.

3 Brush the surface of the disc with the oil.

4 Roll the dough into a cylinder.

5 Coil it up like a snail.

6 Dust the rolling pin with the flour and roll the dough until flat, measuring about 6 inches (15 cm) in diameter. Set the dough aside on a baking sheet. Repeat Step 2–6 for the rest of the dough.

Chapter 2

Soups

A traditional Chinese meal is incomplete without a bowl of nourishing and soothing Chinese soup. Soup is an important part of Chinese cooking and there are a variety of them to explore: soupy, starchy, medicinal, herbal, etc. In the United States, the most popular Chinese soups are made with easy to find and recognizable ingredients, such as eggs, sweet corn, and tofu. In this chapter, you will find some of the most common soups served at Chinese restaurants: Simple Egg Drop Soup (page 53), Hot and Sour Soup (page 55) and Shrimp Wonton Soup (page 56).

West Lake Beef Soup Xi Hu Niu Rou Geng

West Lake Beef Soup, or *xi hu niu rou geng*, is a traditional soup dish from Hangzhou, China. Legend has it that the appearance of the eggy soup resembles the surface of the picturesque West Lake in Hangzhou, and hence the name West Lake Beef Soup. The distinctive taste of this soup comes from the chopped coriander leaves (cilantro), which is added towards the end of the cooking process. The heat diminishes their flavor quickly and the soup is infused with the subtle, citrusy tinge of the coriander leaves (cilantro).

Serves 4 as part of a multicourse meal

6 oz (175 g) ground beef
½ tablespoon Chinese rice wine or sherry
½ teaspoon sesame oil
2½ tablespoons cornstarch
3 tablespoons water
1¾ cups (425 ml) Homemade Chicken Stock (page 31) or 1 can (14 oz/400 g) store-bought chicken broth
1½ cups (375 ml) water
3 dashes white pepper
½ teaspoon salt or to taste
2 large eggs, lightly beaten
⅓ cup (10 g) coarsely chopped coriander leaves (cilantro)

1 Marinate the ground beef with the Chinese rice wine and sesame oil, about 10 minutes. Break up the ground beef into small pieces using a fork after marinating.

2 Mix the cornstarch with 3 tablespoons of water in a small bowl. Stir to blend well. Set aside.

3 Bring the chicken broth and water to a boil in a pot. Lower the heat to medium and add the ground beef into the soup. Skim off the foam on the surface.

4 Add the white pepper and salt, and thicken the soup with the cornstarch mixture. Stir the soup with a ladle and turn off the heat.

5 Swirl the beaten eggs into the soup and immediately stir it three times with a pair of chopsticks. Cover the pot with its lid for 2 minutes. The eggs should be cooked and will form into silken threads. Add the coriander leaves into the soup and stir to blend.

6 Dish out into individual serving bowls and serve immediately.

Sweet Corn and Chicken Soup Su Mi Ji Rou Tang

My friends' two-year-old son is a huge fan of sweet corn and minced chicken soup. It's the only Chinese soup he would eat without spitting it out. Come to think about it, this soup is family friendly, especially for kids. The creamy sweet corn and minced chicken combinations produce a light-tasting soup that's easy on the palate, plus it's healthy and nutritional. Try this soup on some children, and if none are available I am certain you won't mind savoring a bowl or two yourself.

Serves 4 as part of a multicourse meal

2 tablespoons cornstarch
3 tablespoons water
6 oz (175 g) ground chicken
1¾ cups (425 ml) Homemade Chicken Stock (page 31) or 1 can (14-oz/400-g) store-bought chicken broth
1½ cups (375 ml) water
1 can (8¼ oz/250 g) creamy sweet corn
3 dashes white pepper
½ teaspoon salt or to taste
2 large eggs, lightly beaten
Coriander leaves (cilantro), to garnish

1 Mix the cornstarch with 3 tablespoons of water in a small bowl. Stir to blend well. Set aside.
2 Break up the ground chicken into small pieces using a fork.
3 Bring to boil the chicken broth and water in a pot. Lower the heat to medium and add the ground chicken into the soup. Skim off the foam on the surface.
4 Add the creamy sweet corn, white pepper, salt, and thicken the soup with the cornstarch mixture. Stir the soup with a ladle and turn off the heat.
5 Swirl the beaten eggs into the soup and immediately stir three times with a pair of chopsticks. Cover the pot with its lid for 2 minutes. The eggs should be cooked and will form into silken threads.
6 Dish out into individual serving bowls and sprinkle with the coriander leaves. Serve immediately.

Pork Dumpling Soup Siu Kow

Siu kow is the Cantonese pronunciation of dumplings, or *shui jiao* in Chinese. In English, it literally translates to "water dumplings"—which in this case, it's aptly named because the dish is commonly served as a soup dish at Cantonese noodle shops or delis. I love Pork Dumpling (Siu Kow) Soup and often have it at Sam Woo Restaurant, which has a few branches in the Los Angeles Metro Area. Their *siu kow* is legendary—filled with the perfect ratio of ground pork, shrimp, water chestnuts, and wood ear mushrooms. Every bite is savory, luscious, and crunchy. In my research for this recipe I enjoyed countless servings of the delicious *Siu Kow* soup at Sam Woo Restaurant.

Makes 12–20 dumplings or serves 4–6 as part of a
   multicourse meal

1 pack store-bought siu kow or wonton wrappers
4 cups (1 liter) water
1 green onion (scallion), trimmed and cut into
   small rounds, to garnish

Filling
1 small wood ear mushroom
6 oz (175 g) ground pork
4 oz (100 g) shelled and deveined raw shrimp, cut
   into small pieces
2 peeled fresh or canned water chestnuts, minced
1 tablespoon finely chopped green onion (scallion)
1½ teaspoons oil
1 teaspoon Chinese rice wine or sherry
½ teaspoon sesame oil
¾ teaspoon chicken bouillon powder
½ teaspoon fish sauce
½ teaspoon salt
3 dashes white pepper

Soup
1¾ cups (425 ml) Homemade Chicken Stock
   (page 31) or 1 can (14 oz/400 g) store-bought
   chicken broth
1 cup (250 ml) water
3 dashes white pepper
Salt, to taste

> **COOK'S NOTE:** There are different sizes of *siu kow* or wonton wrappers in the market. Use 1 teaspoon of the Filling if the wrappers are smaller, which yields more dumplings.

Pork Dumpling Soup

1 Make the Filling by soaking the wood ear mushroom in warm water for about 15 minutes. Cut it into thin strips.

2 Combine the wood ear mushroom and all the Filling ingredients. Chill the Filling in the refrigerator for 30 minutes.

3 To assemble the dumplings, place a piece of the wrapper on your palm and spoon about 1 tablespoon of the Filling onto the wrapper. Do not overfill. Dip your index finger into a small bowl of water and circle around the outer edges of the dumpling wrapper. Fold the dumpling over and finish by pressing the edges with your thumb and index finger to ensure that the dumpling is sealed tightly and there is no leakage. Repeat for the remaining wrappers and Filling.

4 Place the dumplings on a floured surface or baking sheet. Cover them with a damp kitchen towel to prevent drying.

5 Bring the water to a boil in a pot. Gently transfer the wrapped dumplings into the boiling water and boil until they float to the top, about 2–3 minutes. You may have to boil the dumplings in more than 1 batch, according to the size of your pot.

6 Remove the dumplings with a slotted spoon, drain the excess water, and cover them to prevent drying.

7 Make the soup by bringing the chicken broth and water to a boil in a pot. Add the white pepper and salt to taste.

8 Transfer 3–4 dumplings into a soup bowl, add some of the Soup into the bowl, garnish with some chopped green onion and serve immediately.

Simple Egg Drop Soup   Dan Hua Tang

To be brutally honest—I have never tasted a really decent egg drop soup in the Chinese restaurants here in the United States. So whenever I dine out, I typically avoid the goopy and MSG-laden egg drop soups that are so common here. This all changed when I had egg drop soup at a little restaurant called Jesse, frequented by Chinese food connoisseurs in Shanghai, China. The egg drop soup served at Jesse was so mild and refreshing, and had the sweet tang of fresh tomatoes. My recipe closely replicates the version I was served in Shanghai but slightly thickened with cornstarch. It's eggy, soothing, and comforting, especially on a cold day.

Serves 4 as part of a multicourse meal

2 tablespoons cornstarch
3 tablespoons water
1¾ cups (425 ml) Homemade Chicken Stock (page 31) or 1 can (14-oz/400-g) store-bought chicken broth
1 cup (250 ml) water
½ tomato, diced
3 dashes white pepper
½ teaspoon salt or to taste
2 large eggs, lightly beaten

1 Mix the cornstarch with 3 tablespoons of water in a small bowl. Stir to blend well. Set aside.

2 Bring the chicken broth and water to a boil in a pot. Add the tomato, white pepper, salt, and thicken the soup with the cornstarch mixture. Stir the soup with a ladle and turn off the heat.

3 Swirl the beaten eggs into the soup and immediately stir three times with a pair of chopsticks. Cover the pot with its lid for 2 minutes. The eggs should be cooked and will form into silken threads.

4 Dish out into individual serving bowls and serve immediately.

Mixed Seafood and Tofu Soup
Hai Xian Dou Fu Tang

I am a seafood fanatic and this Mixed Seafood with Tofu Soup has all my favorite seafoods—shrimp, crab meat, and scallops swimming in a mild-tasting broth, flavored with tofu, egg whites, and straw mushrooms. The yellow chives add a Cantonese touch to this seafood soup. It also imbues it with an enticing garlicky aroma. If you can't find yellow chives where you are, you can substitute it with regular green onions. If you have some Chinese black vinegar, drizzle a few drops into the soup for an even richer and piquant overtone.

Serves 4 as part of a multicourse meal

2 tablespoons cornstarch
3 tablespoons water
1¾ cups (425 ml) Homemade Chicken Stock (page 31) or 1 can (14-oz/400-g) store-bought chicken broth
1½ cups (375 ml) water
½ cup (50 g) store-bought frozen peas and carrots
2 oz (50 g) shelled and deveined raw shrimp, cut into small pieces
2 oz (50 g) frozen crabmeat
2 oz (50 g) raw bay scallops
2 oz (50 g) canned straw mushrooms, rinsed and cut into thin slices
4 oz (100 g) soft tofu, rinsed and cut into small cubes
1 tablespoon Chinese rice wine or sherry
½ teaspoon sesame oil
½ teaspoon salt or to taste
3 dashes white pepper
2 egg whites, lightly beaten
1 oz (25 g) yellow chives, cut into 2 in lengths (optional), to garnish

1 Mix the cornstarch with 3 tablespoons of water in a small bowl. Stir to blend well. Set aside.
2 Bring the chicken broth and water to a boil in a pot. Add the frozen peas and carrots, shrimp, crabmeat, bay scallops, straw mushrooms, tofu, and cook for 5 minutes. Season the soup with the Chinese rice wine, sesame oil, salt, and pepper. Thicken the soup with the cornstarch mixture. Stir the soup with a ladle and turn off the heat.
3 Swirl the beaten eggs into the soup and immediately stir it three times with a pair of chopsticks. Cover the pot with its lid for 2 minutes. The eggs should be cooked and will form into silken threads.
4 Add the yellow chives (if using) into the soup and serve immediately.

Hot and Sour Soup Suan La Tang

Hot and Sour Soup is Sichuan in origin. Situated in the southwestern part of China, the province of Sichuan is famed for its fiery hot cuisine. This Hot and Sour Soup is, therefore, piquant, peppery (from the white pepper), and sharp (from the tartness of the Chinese vinegars).

I love to zest up my Hot and Sour Soup with some homemade Chili Oil (page 27), which not only adds a nice red sheen to the soup, but also makes it even more appetizing.

Serves 6 as part of a multicourse meal

4 oz (100 g) pork, cut into thin strips
½ teaspoon Chinese rice wine or sherry
1 teaspoon cornstarch
1 large wood ear mushroom
1¾ cups (425 ml) Homemade Chicken Stock
   (page 31) or 1 can (14 oz/400 g) store-bought
   chicken broth
1½ cups (375 ml) water
½ small carrot, cut into thin matchstick strips
4 oz (100 g) soft or medium tofu, rinsed and cut
   into strips
2 oz (50 g) canned bamboo shoots, rinsed and cut
   into thin matchstick strips
1 large egg, lightly beaten
1 green onion (scallion), trimmed and cut into
   small rounds, to garnish

Seasonings
1 tablespoon soy sauce
1 tablespoon Chinese black vinegar or to taste
1½ teaspoons Chinese rice vinegar or to taste
½ heaping teaspoon white pepper
¼ teaspoon salt or to taste
2 tablespoons cornstarch
3 tablespoons water
½ tablespoon Chili Oil (page 27) or to taste

1 Marinate the pork with the rice wine and cornstarch, about 15 minutes.
2 Soak the wood ear mushroom in warm water, about 15 minutes. Cut into thin strips.
3 Mix all the ingredients for the Seasonings in a small bowl. Set aside.
4 Bring to boil the chicken broth and water in a pot. Add the pork, wood ear mushroom, carrot, tofu, and bamboo shoots. Continue to boil, about 5 minutes.
5 Skim off the foam. Add the Seasonings into the soup, stir with a ladle and turn off the heat.
6 Swirl the beaten egg into the soup and immediately stir three times with a pair of chopsticks. Cover the pot with its lid for 2 minutes. The egg should be cooked and will form into silken threads.
7 Dish out into individual serving bowls and garnish with the green onion. Serve immediately.

Shrimp Wonton Soup Xia Hun Tun Tang

A few years ago, while traveling in Hong Kong, I chanced upon a mom-and-pop noodle joint that served the best shrimp wontons in the world. As simple as it sounds, finding perfect shrimp wontons with the right texture, ample filling, and great taste is not that easy these days.

Great shrimp wontons should be tightly packed into the wrapper and the shrimp has to be fresh, big (always a plus), and most of all, its texture has to be crunchy so every bite of the shrimp just "bounces" in the mouth, as the Cantonese would say. To ensure the best result for this recipe, please follow the tips on "How to Make Shrimp Bouncy" on page 13. The difference between a well-treated shrimp and "limpy" shrimp is the difference between heaven and earth in this classic Cantonese recipe.

Makes 20 wontons or serves 6 as part of a
  multicourse meal

20 store-bought wonton wrappers
4 cups (1 liter) water
1 green onion (scallion), trimmed and cut
  into small rounds, to garnish

Filling
8 oz (250 g) shelled and deveined
  medium-sized raw shrimp
1 tablespoon chopped yellow chives
  (½ in/1.25 cm lengths)
1 teaspoon oil
¼ teaspoon salt
¼ teaspoon chicken bouillon powder
¼ teaspoon fish sauce
½ teaspoon Chinese rice wine or sherry
¼ teaspoon sugar
½ teaspoon sesame oil
3 dashes white pepper
½ teaspoon oil

Soup
1¾ cups (425 ml) Homemade Chicken
  Stock (page 00) or 1 can (14 oz/400 g)
  store-bought chicken broth
1 cup (250 ml) water
3 dashes white pepper
Salt, to taste

1 To make the Filling, treat the shrimp according to "How to Make Shrimp Bouncy" on Page 13.

2 Cut ²/3 portion of the shrimp into 3–4 pieces in equal lengths and set aside. Smash and pound the remaining ¹/3 portion of the shrimp using the back of a Chinese cleaver and then coarsely mince it with the cleaver a few times (refer to the picture guide on page 29). Alternatively, you can use a food processor to mince the ¹/3 portion of the shrimp.

3 Combining all the shrimp and the rest of the ingredients together. Chill the Filling in the refrigerator for 30 minutes.

4 Assemble the Shrimp Wontons by following the instructional guide on page 57.

5 Bring the water to a boil in a pot. Gently transfer the wrapped wontons into the boiling water and boil until the wontons float to the top, about 2–3 minutes. You may have to boil the wontons in more than 1 batch, depending on the size of your pot.

6 Remove the wontons with a slotted spoon, drain the excess water, and cover them to prevent drying.

7 To make the Soup, bring to boil the chicken broth and water in a pot. Add the white pepper and salt to taste.

8 Transfer 3–4 wontons into a small soup bowl, add some of the Soup into the bowl, garnish with some chopped green onion (scallion) and serve immediately.

HOW TO WRAP THE SHRIMP WONTONS

1 Place a piece of wonton wrapper on a flat surface, spoon about 1 heaping teaspoon of the Filling onto the wrapper. Do not overfill. Dip your index finger into a small bowl of water and circle around the outer edges of the wonton wrapper.

2 Fold over to form a triangle shape, press to seal the edges tightly.

3 Using both thumbs and index fingers, bring the two corners together and secure them firmly. (One corner should be above the other.) Dab on a little water to help seal it.

4 Place the wrapped wontons on a floured surface or baking sheet. Cover the wontons to prevent drying.

Chapter 3

Dim Sum and Dumplings

When it comes to Chinese food, Cantonese cuisine is probably my first love, and, naturally, dim sum ranks very high in my Chinese food hierarchy. And then I discovered Chinese dumplings while traveling in China and became an instant and ardent fan at the very first bite. Now, both dim sum and dumplings are two of my favorite Chinese foods!

Imagine trays upon trays of bamboo steamers, with billowing clouds of steam, each carrying fresh, delicate, and succulent dim sum; an assortment of steamed buns, deep-fried, and baked little bites; scrumptious dumplings filled with meat, vegetables, and/or seafood. Dim sum and dumplings are practically begging to be eaten! In this chapter, you will find some of the most popular dim sum and dumpling recipes that are sure to satisfy your appetite.

Crispy Shrimp Dumplings

I was 18 when I first tasted these Crispy Shrimp Dumplings. My late grandmother, late parents, aunt, my brother, and I visited my uncle and his family in Hong Kong. My uncle is a huge foodie, so much so that his office was located right above a renowned dim sum restaurant, which, not coincidentally, was his favorite restaurant in Hong Kong.

Every day during our stay, my uncle would treat us to the immaculate dim sum served at this restaurant. Crispy Shrimp Dumplings, called *meng har gok* in Cantonese, were always on our order list. Served with a mayonnaise dipping sauce, these fried dumplings remain my favorite dim sum.

Makes 12 or serves 4 as an appetizer, snack, or dim sum

12 store-bought wonton wrappers
4 tablespoons mayonnaise, for dipping

Filling
8 oz (250 g) shelled and deveined medium-sized raw shrimp
1 tablespoon finely chopped green onion (scallion)
¼ teaspoon salt
¼ teaspoon fish sauce
¼ teaspoon chicken bouillon powder
½ teaspoon sesame oil
½ teaspoon Chinese rice wine or sherry
¼ teaspoon sugar
3 dashes white pepper
½ teaspoon oil

> **COOK'S NOTE:** If you have problems sealing the dumpling, dip your index finger into a small bowl of water and circle around the outer edges of the wonton wrapper to help seal it.

1 To make the Filling, treat the shrimp according to "How to Make Shrimp Bouncy" on page 13. This is an optional step.

2 Cut ⅔ portion of the shrimp into 4 pieces in equal lengths. Smash and pound the remaining ⅓ portion of the shrimp using the back of a Chinese cleaver and then mince it with the cleaver a few times (refer to the picture guide on page 29). Alternatively, you can use a food processor to mince the ⅓ portion of the shrimp.

3 Combine the shrimp and the rest of the Filling ingredients together. Chill the Filling in the refrigerator for 30 minutes.

4 Assemble the shrimp dumpling by following the instructional picture guide on page 61.

5 Heat 2 to 3 inches (5 to 7.5 cm) of the oil in a wok or stockpot to 350°F (175°C) for deep-frying. Gently drop the shrimp dumplings into the oil and deep fry in batches.

6 Deep-fry until they turn golden brown. Dish out with a strainer or slotted spoon, draining the excess oil by laying the Crispy Shrimp Dumplings on a wire rack or a dish lined with paper towels. Serve immediately with the mayonnaise.

HOW TO WRAP THE SHRIMP DUMPLINGS

1 Place a piece of wonton wrapper on a flat surface, spoon about 1 tablespoon of the Filling onto the wrapper. Do not overfill.

2 Fold over to form a triangle shape.

3 Using the thumbs and index fingers of both hands, press and squeeze both sides of the dumpling towards the center to form the folds. Make sure the shrimp dumpling is sealed tightly and there is no leakage.

4 Place the wrapped shrimp dumplings on a floured surface or baking sheet. Cover the dumplings to prevent drying.

Sweet Pork Buns

By now, America and the world should be familiar with these pork buns, made famous lately by celebrity chef David Chang of Momofuku in New York City. This pork bun recipe makes good use of the Crispy Roast Pork recipe on page 76. Stuff a piece of this roast meat inside a store-bought Chinese steamed bun, garnish with some fresh cucumber, green onion (scallion), flavor it with hoisin sauce and you will have a scrumptious and filling dim sum or afternoon snack. It's also great to serve these buns at a dim sum party where your guests can assemble them to their liking.

If you can't find traditional Chinese steamed buns, you can substitute with Pillsbury's biscuit dough. Fold the biscuit dough in half and steam until they turn fluffy. It's that easy!

Makes 8 or serves 4 as an appetizer, snack, or dim sum

Store-bought Chinese steamed buns
3 tablespoons hoisin sauce
½ small cucumber, peeled and cut into thin matchstick strips
1 lb (500 g) Crispy Roast Pork (page 76), cut into 8 pieces
1 green onion (scallion), trimmed and cut into thin threads
Some coriander leaves (cilantro)

1 Steam the Chinese steamed buns until they become soft and puffy, about 5 minutes.
2 Flip open the steamed bun carefully and spread some hoisin sauce on both sides of the bun.
3 Slide some cucumber strips inside the bun, and then place a piece of the Roast Pork in the center of the bun.
4 Top the Roast pork with some green onion and coriander leaves.
5 Fold up the buns and serve immediately.

Baked BBQ Pork Puffs   Cha Shao Su

Cantonese BBQ Pork (page 81)—*char siu*—is a versatile and highly adaptable ingredient. It can be eaten as is, as a side ingredient for fried rice or noodle dishes, or as a filling for steamed *char siu bao* (barbeque pork buns) or these Baked BBQ Pork Puffs speckled with sesame seeds. Traditionally, Cantonese chefs would spend hours making the perfect, flaky, and crumbly water and oil dough. For my recipe, I use store-bought puff pastry and achieve an equally impressive result.

COOK'S NOTES: If you don't like coriander leaves (cilantro), feel free to use green onion (scallion).

Dust the fork and your hands with some all-purpose flour for easy handling in case the puff pastry is too soft and sticky.

If the puff pastry is too dry, dab a little water around the edges of the puff pastry to help sealing.

Makes 10 or serves 3 as an appetizer, snack, or dim sum

2 sheets store-bought puff pastry
2 egg yolks, lightly beaten for egg wash
3 tablespoons white sesame seeds

Filling
8 oz (250 g) Cantonese BBQ Pork (page 81), diced into small pieces
3 tablespoons Chinese BBQ Sauce (page 29)
½ tablespoon chopped coriander leaves (cilantro)
½ teaspoon white sesame seeds

1 Thaw the puff pastry according to the package instructions.
2 Heat up a wok or skillet over medium heat. Cook all the ingredients in the Filling until the sauce becomes thick and sticky. Dish out the Filling and let cool.
3 Cut the puff pastry sheets into 4-inch (10 cm) squares.
4 Add about 1 heaping tablespoon of the Filling to the center of the puff pastry. Fold the puff pastry over to form a triangle. Do not overfill. Seal the edges tightly by pressing firmly with your fingers. Make sure there is no leakage. After sealing, use a knife to cut the uneven edges to form a uniform triangle. Use the back of the fork to make a pattern around the edges. Brush the top of the puff with some egg wash. Sprinkle the white sesame seeds on top and place the puffs on a baking sheet.
5 Preheat the oven to 350°F (175°C) and bake the puffs until they turn golden brown, about 20–25 minutes. Serve hot.

Classic Spring Rolls   Chun Juan

The spring roll is probably one of the most iconic foods in Chinese cuisine, but also one that's extensively—and sometimes, crudely—adapted. Almost every country in Asia has its own interpretation of spring rolls: *lumpia* in Indonesia and the Philippines, *cha gio* in Vietnam, and *popiah* in Malaysia and Singapore. In the United States, they are known as egg rolls—which is a chunky version of this recipe that's stuffed primarily with antibiotic-tasting shredded cabbage, and wrapped with thick wonton skins! Even in China, spring rolls come in a variety of fillings and each region has its own version, so much so that it's almost difficult to define the best spring roll recipe! Despite infinite varieties, good spring rolls never fail to tantalize the taste buds. This is my take on the Chinese spring rolls, inspired by my favorite Chinese restaurant. They are moist, juicy, and packed with an assortment of ingredients that make a perfect filling.

Makes 24 or serves 6 as an appetizer, snack, or
  dim sum

1 large egg, lightly beaten for egg wash
24 store-bought spring roll wrappers, 8 in (20
  cm) square in size
Oil, for deep-frying

Filling
1 teaspoon cornstarch
1 teaspoon Chinese rice wine or sherry
4 oz (100 g) pork butt/leg, cut into thin
  matchstick strips
2 tablespoons oil
2 oz (50 g) raw shrimp, coarsely chopped
3 dried shiitake mushrooms, soaked until
  soft, stems discarded, caps diced
4 oz (100 g) cabbage, thinly sliced
½ small carrot, cut into thin matchstick strips
1 green onion (scallion), trimmed and cut into
  small rounds

Seasonings
½ tablespoon oyster sauce
1 teaspoon dark soy sauce
¼ teaspoon sesame oil
3 dashes white pepper
¼ teaspoon sugar
¼ teaspoon chicken bouillon powder
¼ cup (65 ml) water
¼ teaspoon salt

1 Mix all the ingredients for the Seasonings in a bowl and set aside.
2 To make the Filling, combine the cornstarch and rice wine in a bowl large enough to hold the pork. Marinate the pork for about 15 minutes.
3 Heat the oil in a wok or skillet over high heat. Add the shrimp, pork, and stir-fry until they are half cooked. Add the remaining ingredients and the Seasonings. Stir-fry until the Filling is cooked and becomes somewhat dry. (Wet filling will make the spring rolls too soft.) Dish out and let cool.
4 Assemble the spring rolls by following the instructional picture guide on page 65.
5 Heat 2 to 3 inches (5 to 7.5 cm) of the oil in a wok or stockpot to 350°F (175°C) for deep-frying. Gently drop the spring rolls into the oil and deep fry in batches. Deep-fry until they turn light golden brown. Dish out with a strainer or slotted spoon, draining the excess oil by laying the spring rolls on a wire rack or a dish lined with paper towels. Serve immediately as is or with chili dipping sauce.

HOW TO WRAP THE SPRING ROLLS

1 Place a piece of spring roll wrapper on a flat surface, spread about 2 tablespoons of the Filling lengthwise onto the center of the wrapper. Do not overfill. Using a small brush or your index finger, dab the egg wash around the outer edges of the wrapper.

2 Fold the bottom side of the wrapper over the Filling.

3 Then fold the left and right sides of the wrapper over the Filling. Make sure the Filling is packed tightly.
4 Roll the spring roll over until it reaches the other end of the wrapper.

5 Make sure the spring roll is sealed tightly and there is no leakage. Repeat until all the wrappers and Filling are used up.

Delicious Pot Stickers Guo Tie

My Chinese friends from mainland China introduced me to dumplings—the much-loved morsels of ground meat and vegetables wrapped with dough skin. Dumplings are a staple of Chinese cuisine, especially in Northern China. The best dumplings are the ones that are lusciously plump, thin-skinned, and stuffed with just the right amount of filling.

There are many types of dumplings: boiled, pan-fried, steamed, or deep-fried. The most-loved is probably the pot sticker, *Guo Tie*. Pot stickers are easy to make—wrapped with store-bought dumpling wrappers or homemade wrappers (recipe on page 31), pan-fried to a golden brown, and then lightly steamed with water.

Pot stickers are versatile because so many different proteins can be used: ground pork, chicken, turkey, beef, fish, or shrimp. Vegetables, such as chopped cabbage or Chinese (Napa) cabbage, are often added to further enhance the taste. The best pot stickers I've had are the ones served at *Manjia Fantian* or Mao's Restaurant in Beijing—with their unforgettable texture and flavor they were pure perfection!

Makes 20 dumplings or serves 4 as an appetizer or snack

20 store-bought pot sticker wrappers or Homemade Dumpling Wrappers (page 31)
1½ tablespoons oil
½ cup (125 ml) water
Dumpling Dipping Sauce (page 71), for dipping

Filling
8 oz (250 g) ground pork
4 oz (100 g) shelled and deveined medium-sized raw shrimp
½ cup (80 g) thinly sliced Chinese (Napa) cabbage, squeezed of excess water
2 tablespoons finely chopped green onion (scallion)
One 1 in (2.5 cm) piece fresh ginger, peeled and grated
1 teaspoon Chinese rice wine or sherry
½ teaspoon sesame oil
½ teaspoon salt
3 dashes white pepper

1 Make the Filling by combining all the ingredients together. Chill the Filling in the refrigerator for 30 minutes.
2 Assemble the pot stickers by following the instructional picture guide on the right.
3 Heat the oil in a skillet over medium heat. Arrange the dumplings on the skillet and cover with its lid. Pan-fry the pot stickers until the bottoms turn golden brown and become crispy.
4 Add the water and cover the skillet with its lid immediately. The water should sizzle and steam the pot stickers. Turn the heat to low as soon as the water has completely evaporated. Cook the pot stickers for another 2 minutes, dish out and serve hot with the Dumpling Dipping Sauce.

HOW TO WRAP THE POT STICKERS OR DUMPLINGS

1 Place a piece of the wrapper on your palm and spoon about 1 heaping teaspoon of the Filling onto the wrapper. Do not overfill. Dip your index finger into a small bowl of water and moisten the outer edges of the wrapper.

2 Fold the pot sticker over to form a half moon shape. Press and seal only the middle part of the pot sticker. Leave both sides open for pleating.

3 Use your right thumb and index finger to make a pleat. Pinch to secure it tightly.

4 Repeat the same and make about 3–4 pleats. (Start with 3 pleats if you are a beginner.) Turn the pot sticker around and repeat Step 3.

5 Finish by pressing all the pleats with your thumb and index finger to ensure that the pot sticker is sealed tightly and there is no leakage.

6 A nicely wrapped pot sticker should have a crescent shape.

Makes 20 dumplings or serves 4 as an appetizer or snack

20 store-bought jiaozi or pot sticker wrappers or Homemade Dumpling Wrappers (page 31)
4 cups (1 liter) water, for boiling
½ cup (125 ml) Dumpling Dipping Sauce (page 71), for dipping

Filling
8 oz (250 g) ground pork
2 oz (50 g) fresh garlic chives, cut into small pieces
1 teaspoon Chinese rice wine or sherry
¼ teaspoon salt
¼ teaspoon sesame oil
1 teaspoon soy sauce
½ teaspoon cornstarch
3 dashes white pepper

1 Make the Filling by combining all the ingredients together. Chill the Filling in the refrigerator for 30 minutes.
2 To assemble the Pork and Chive Dumpling, place a piece of dumpling wrapper on your palm and spoon about 1 heaping teaspoon of the Filling onto the wrapper. Do not overfill. Dip your index finger into a small bowl of water and circle around the outer edges of the dumpling wrapper. Fold the dumpling over to form a half-moon shape. Finish by pressing the edges with your thumb and index finger to ensure that the dumpling is sealed tightly and there is no leakage. Repeat the same for the remaining wrappers and Filling.
3 Place the dumplings on a floured surface or baking sheet. Cover them with a damp kitchen towel to prevent drying.
4 Bring the water to a boil in a pot. Gently transfer the wrapped dumplings into the boiling water and boil until the dumplings float to the top, about 3 minutes.
5 Remove the dumplings with a slotted spoon, draining the excess water, then serve immediately with the Dumpling Dipping Sauce.

Pork and Chive Dumplings

The dumpling is a traditional dish in Northern China. Known as *jiaozi* in Chinese, dumplings can be served anytime of the day: breakfast, lunch, dinner, or as a light snack. In fact, in Northern China, wheat-based foods such as dumplings, noodles, and bread often replace steamed rice as the main part of the meal.

In Beijing, there are many dumpling restaurants that offer *jiaozi*. My favorite restaurant is *Tianjin Bai Jiao Yuan*, a humble but buzzing neighborhood dumpling house that serves up to hundreds of delectable northern-style dumplings with pork, beef, shrimp, crab, sea cucumber, mantis prawn, and salted egg yolk as fillings. Made with the most basic ingredients of ground pork and chive, this Pork and Chive Dumplings recipe reminds me of my many eating trips at *Tianjin Bai Jiao Yuan*.

Steamed Chicken and Mushroom Dumplings

The mental image of steamed dumplings—especially when they are fresh out of the steamer with little beads of "sweat" dotting their surface—always makes my stomach rumble and my mouth water. Regardless of the filling, steamed dumplings are always a treat for the taste buds. This Steamed Chicken and Mushroom Dumplings recipe pairs two common ingredients into heavenly morsels. Dip the piping hot dumplings in the Dumpling Dipping Sauce (page 71), or eat them as is.

Makes 20 dumplings or serves 4–6 as an appetizer or snack

20 store-bought pot sticker wrappers or Homemade Dumpling Wrappers (page 31)
½ cup water (125 ml), for steaming
½ cup (125 ml) Dumpling Dipping Sauce (page 71), for dipping

Filling
2 dried shiitake mushrooms
10 oz (330 g) skinless, boneless chicken thighs
½ cup (80 g) thinly sliced cabbage
1 green onion (scallion), finely chopped
1 tablespoon Chinese rice wine or sherry
½ teaspoon salt
1 tablespoon soy sauce
½ teaspoon sesame oil
3 dashes white pepper

1 To make the Filling, soak the dried shiitake mushrooms in warm water until they become soft. Squeeze the mushrooms dry, discard the stems, cut and dice the caps into tiny pieces.
2 Grind the chicken thighs to a fine paste in a food processor.
3 Combine the mushrooms and ground chicken with the rest of the ingredients. Chill the Filling in the refrigerator for 30 minutes.
4 Assemble the dumplings by following the instructional picture guide (page 67).
5 Arrange the dumplings in a bamboo steamer (lined with parchment paper) and steam for 6–8 minutes or until cooked. You may have to steam the dumplings in more than 1 batch, depending on the size of your steamer.
6 Serve the steamed dumplings immediately with Dumpling Dipping Sauce.

Shrimp and Yellow Chive Dumplings

My favorite dumpling restaurant, Dumpling 10053, located in El Monte, California, inspires this recipe. This little dumpling joint serves perfect Shrimp and Yellow Chive Dumplings. Yellow chives are not commonly available in regular supermarkets, so you can adapt the recipe using the regular Chinese chives or garlic chives, or even green onion, which is just as tasty. I prefer my Homemade Dumpling Wrappers (page 31) for this recipe because the texture of the wrapper is just better overall.

Makes 20 or serves 6 as an appetizer or snack

20 store-bought jiaozi or pot sticker wrappers or Homemade Dumpling Wrappers (page 31)
4 cups (1 liter) water, for boiling
½ cup (125 ml) Dumpling Dipping Sauce (below), for dipping

Filling
8 oz (250 g) shelled and deveined medium-sized raw shrimp
1 tablespoon chopped yellow chives (½ in/1.25 cm lengths)
1 teaspoon oil
¼ teaspoon salt
¼ teaspoon chicken bouillon powder
¼ teaspoon fish sauce
½ teaspoon Chinese rice wine or sherry
¼ teaspoon sugar
½ teaspoon sesame oil
3 dashes white pepper
½ teaspoon oil

1 To make the Filling, treat the shrimp according to "How to Make Shrimp Bouncy" on page 13. This is an optional step.

2 Cut $^2/_3$ portion of the shrimp into 4 pieces in equal lengths. Smash and pound the remaining $^1/_3$ portion of the shrimp using the back of a Chinese cleaver and then mince it with the cleaver a few times (refer to picture guide on page 29). Alternatively, you can use a food processor to mince the $^1/_3$ portion of the shrimp.

3 Combine the shrimp and all the ingredients together. Chill the Filling in the refrigerator for 30 minutes.

4 To assemble the Shrimp and Yellow Chive Dumpling, place a piece of dumpling wrapper on your palm and spoon about 1 heaping teaspoon of the Filling onto the wrapper. Do not overfill. Dip your index finger into a small bowl of water and circle around the outer edges of the dumpling wrapper. Fold the dumpling over to form a half-moon shape. Finish by pressing the edges with your thumb and index finger to ensure that the dumpling is sealed tightly and there is no leakage. Repeat the same for the remaining wrappers and Filling. Place the dumplings on a floured surface or baking sheet. Cover them with a damp kitchen towel to prevent drying.

5 Bring the water to a boil in a pot. Gently transfer the wrapped dumplings into the boiling water and boil until the dumplings float to the top, about 3 minutes.

6 Remove the dumplings with a slotted spoon, draining the excess water, then serve immediately with the Dumpling Dipping Sauce.

Dumpling Dipping Sauce

Chinese dumplings are commonly served with a black Chinese vinegar dipping sauce, which pairs wonderfully with the savory taste of steamed, boiled, pan-fried, or deep-fried dumplings. This is a basic Dumpling Dipping Sauce that goes well with Delicious Pot Stickers (page 66), Pork and Chive Dumplings (page 68), and Steamed Chicken and Mushroom Dumplings (page 69). Add slivers of fresh young ginger and Chili Oil (optional) to give an extra punch to the dipping sauce.

Makes ½ cup (125 ml)

½ cup (125 ml) Chinese black vinegar
2 tablespoons soy sauce
1 teaspoon store-bought or homemade Chili Oil (page 27) (optional)

One 1½ in (3.75 cm) piece fresh young ginger, peeled and cut into fine matchstick strips (optional)

1 Combine the Chinese black vinegar with soy sauce in a small bowl. Add the chili oil, if using, into the sauce. Stir to blend well.

2 Pour the sauce into individual saucers and add the ginger, if using. Serve the sauce as a condiment with dumplings.

Siu Mai

When it comes to Cantonese dim sum, Siu Mai is the epitome of goodness and a must-have item on your dim sum menu. Made with pork and shrimp and neatly folded up in a nice parcel, Siu Mai is a mouthful of pure gastronomical bliss—fresh, juicy, and delightful. To create the best homemade Siu Mai recipe, I studied and scrutinized the texture of the siu mai served at all my favorite dim sum restaurants. There is one thing my recipe has in common with them all: using shredded pork in small pieces or strips (not the ground pork). This marriage of shrimp and shredded pork is the perfect combination because of the resulting texture (a highly regarded aspect of quality dim sum).

Makes 20 or serves 6 as an appetizer, snack, or dim sum

20 store-bought siu mai or wonton
   wrappers

Filling
1 big dried shiitake mushroom
4 oz (100 g) shelled and deveined
   medium-sized raw shrimp
8 oz (250 g) pork butt or pork neck, cut
   into small strips
¾ teaspoon sesame oil
1 teaspoon chicken bouillon powder
1 teaspoon Chinese rice wine or sherry
1 teaspoon cornstarch
1 tablespoon egg white
¼ heaping teaspoon salt
1 teaspoon sugar

Garnishing
Frozen green peas

1 Make the Filling by soaking the dried shiitake mushroom in warm water in a small bowl until it becomes soft. Squeeze the mushroom dry with your hand, discard the stem, cut and dice the mushroom caps into tiny pieces.
2 Cut each shrimp into 4 pieces of equal length. You can treat the shrimp according to "How to Make Shrimp Bouncy" on page 13, an optional step.
3 Combine the mushroom, shrimp, pork and all the Filling ingredients together. Chill the Filling in the refrigerator for 30 minutes.
4 Assemble the Siu Mai by following the instructional picture guide on the right.
5 Arrange the Siu Mai in a bamboo steamer (lined with parchment paper) and steam for 6–8 minutes or until cooked. You may have to steam the Siu Mai in more than 1 batch, depending on the size of your steamer.
6 Serve hot with garlic chili sauce.

HOW TO WRAP THE SIU MAI

1 Place a piece of siu mai or wonton wrapper on your palm and spoon about 1 tablespoon of the Filling onto the wrapper.
2 Make a circle with your left thumb and index finger. Place the Siu Mai into the circle. Fold it by gently squeezing with your thumb and index finger.
3 Dab your right index finger with a little water and gently press and smooth out the Filling surface while still holding the Siu Mai in the circle. Make sure the filling is packed tightly.
4 Use a pair of scissors to cut off the exposed and uneven edges of the wrapper (optional).
5 Add a green pea in the middle of the Siu Mai.

Chapter 4

Beef and Pork

My ex-boss, who is Korean, once told me that the Chinese have a way of preparing really delectable pork dishes with scrumptious flavors without the presence of that distinctly "porky" smell. Whenever we traveled to China, she would always order the pork dishes, and she always relished her choice.

Pork is loved by the Chinese people. It's widely consumed and used abundantly in everyday cooking: from soups to stir-fries, roasting to braising, dim sum to dumplings. Without a doubt the Chinese make some of the best pork dishes in the world.

While pork is the protein of choice for the Chinese, beef is also popular, especially to the Muslim minority where pork is forbidden. This chapter covers a number of favorite pork and beef recipes, including the increasingly accepted roast pork dishes and popular beef take-outs.

Crispy Roast Pork Siu Yuk

The Chinese, especially the Cantonese, love roasted meats. In Cantonese cuisine, roasting or barbeque (known as *siu laap*), includes an array of wide offerings. As many of the early Chinese immigrants originated from the Guangdong province in Southern China, *siu laap* had traveled far beyond China and Hong Kong and it's now popular all over the world. Wherever there is a Chinatown, you will be able to find *siu laap*. This Crispy Roast Pork is a well-known and loved Cantonese roast meat dish. The crispy crackling of the meat is highly favored by Chinese food connoisseurs. My recipe is tried and tested and you no longer need to trek to Chinatown for a serving of this crispy meat.

Serves 4 as part of a multicourse meal

2 lbs (1 kg) pork belly
1 teaspoon sea salt, for sprinkling
Oil, for brushing

Marinade
1½ tablespoons soy sauce
½ teaspoon Chinese five spice powder
¼ teaspoon white pepper
¾ teaspoon salt
½ teaspoon sugar

1 Mix all the ingredients for the Marinade in a small bowl. Set aside.
2 Keep the pork belly's skin intact. Scrape the skin surface of the pork belly with a sharp knife to remove any impurities. Rinse and clean well with cold running water. Pat dry with paper towels.
3 Poke the skin evenly and thoroughly using a toothpick or the pointed tip of a bamboo skewer. This will ensure the beehive-like crispy crackling. Wipe off the skin surface with paper towels after you're done.
4 Slit the meat part of the pork belly, about 1 inch (2.5 cm) apart and 3/4 inch (2 cm) deep. Using a small brush, brush the Marinade on the pork and into the slits. Be careful not to get the Marinade on the skin, pat dry with paper towels if you do. Sprinkle the salt evenly on the skin.
5 Marinate the pork for 2–3 hours at room temperature, exposing the skin to allow air-drying. You can also use a fan to air-dry the skin.
6 After marinating, wrap the pork belly tightly with two sheets of aluminum foil, exposing only the pork skin. Heat the oven to 400°F (200°C) and roast for 50 minutes. Take it out and brush the skin surface with the oil. Sprinkle a little more salt on the skin and turn the oven setting to broil. Put the pork belly back into the oven and broil the skin, about 3–5 minutes. Check at the 3–minute mark to make sure it's not burnt.
7 Transfer the pork belly out of the oven, let cool for about 10 minutes. Cut the pork belly into pieces and serve immediately.

Sichuan Twice-Cooked Pork Hui Guo Rou

Whenever I dine at Sichuan restaurants I always order Sichuan Twice-Cooked Pork or *hui guo rou*. I have never once questioned or tried to figure out what was meant by "twice-cooked" or *hui guo* (meaning "returning to wok"). When I was working on this recipe I asked my good friend Mr. Xiong, a restaurateur specializing in Sichuan cuisine, and he taught me the cooking techniques behind this famed Sichuan dish. The "twice-cooked" process basically involved boiling and stir-frying. The pork belly is boiled and sliced into bacon-like thin pieces, and then stir-fried in a wok. Traditionally, Sichuan Twice-Cooked Pork is made with pork belly. If you prefer a healthier version of this dish, you can substitute with pork butt, pork leg, or pork tenderloin.

Serves 3–4 as part of a multicourse meal

10 oz (330 g) pork belly
Water, for boiling
2 teaspoons oil
2 cloves garlic, thinly sliced
2 oz (50 g) leeks, cut diagonally into
    1 in (2.5 cm) lengths
½ small green bell pepper, deseeded
    and cut into pieces
½ small red bell pepper, deseeded and
    cut into pieces
2 oz (50 g) canned thinly sliced
    bamboo shoots, rinsed

Sauce
1½ tablespoons hot bean sauce
1 tablespoon sweet bean sauce
½ teaspoon Chili Oil (page 27)
1 tablespoon soy sauce
¼ teaspoon salt or to taste

1 Remove the skin of the pork belly before boiling it in the water. Boil until cooked, about 10 minutes. Transfer the pork belly out, let it cool, and slice it into bacon-like thin pieces, measuring about 1½ inches (3.75 cm) width by 2 inches (5 cm) length.
2 Mix all the ingredients for the Sauce in a small bowl. Set aside.
3 Heat ½ teaspoon of the oil in a wok or skillet over high heat. Add the pork belly and stir-fry until they are slightly curled.

Dish out and drain the excess oil of the pork belly on a dish lined with paper towels. Let it cool.
4 Heat up the remaining oil in the wok or skillet. Add the garlic and stir-fry until aromatic, and then add the leeks, peppers, and bamboo shoots. Toss the ingredients a few times with the spatula before adding the pork belly and the Sauce.
5 Stir to combine the ingredients well, dish out and serve immediately with steamed rice.

Mongolian Beef Cong Bao Niu Rou

Mongolia's mountainous terrain and harsh climatic conditions shape the diet of its nomadic people. Livestock such as sheep, goats, camels, yaks, cattle, and animal fats are the main source of their food, especially during winter. I once watched a documentary about Mongolia and their staple food certainly doesn't include Mongolian Beef—a stir-fried beef dish with green onion, so I'm not sure where the name comes from. In any case, a great Mongolian Beef dish should be tender, soft, and sweet. I prefer beef flap meat for this dish, but you can use flank steak or beef tenderloin instead. It's critical that you cut the beef across the grain (page 13) to ensure tenderness.

Serves 2 as a main dish with rice or 4 as part of a multicourse meal

8 oz (250 g) beef tenderloin, flank steak or flap meat, cut into pieces
2½ tablespoons oil
2 cloves garlic, minced
One 1 in (2.5 cm) piece fresh ginger, peeled and sliced into thin pieces
3 green onions (scallions), cut into 2 in (5 cm) lengths

Marinade
1 tablespoon soy sauce
1 teaspoon dark soy sauce
½ tablespoon oyster sauce
1 teaspoon hoisin sauce
1 teaspoon Chinese rice wine or sherry
1 teaspoon cornstarch
½ teaspoon sesame oil
1 teaspoon sugar
¼ teaspoon salt
3 dashes white pepper

1 Treat the beef according to "How to Tenderize Meat" on page 13. This is an optional step.
2 Marinate the beef with all the ingredients for the Marinade, about 15 minutes.
3 Heat 1 tablespoon of the oil in a wok or skillet over high heat. Stir-fry the beef until the beef is browned on the outside but still pink inside. Dish out and set aside.
4 Heat the remaining oil in the wok or skillet over high heat. Add the garlic and ginger and stir-fry until aromatic. Transfer the beef into the wok or skillet and stir-fry until the beef is cooked through and the center of the meat is no longer pink, about 1–2 minutes. Add the green onion; stir to combine the ingredients well. Dish out and serve immediately with steamed rice.

Serves 2 as a main dish with rice or 4 as part of a
multicourse meal

8 oz (250 g) beef tenderloin, flank steak or flap
    meat, cut into pieces
2½ tablespoons oil
1 clove garlic, minced
One 1 in (2.5 cm) piece fresh ginger, peeled and
    sliced
½ small green bell pepper, deseeded and cut into
    pieces
½ small red bell pepper, deseeded and cut into
    pieces
½ onion, cut into strips
1 teaspoon freshly ground black pepper
Salt, to taste

Marinade
1½ teaspoons Maggi seasoning sauce
½ teaspoon soy sauce
½ teaspoon dark soy sauce
1 teaspoon oyster sauce
1 teaspoon Worcestershire sauce
1 teaspoon Chinese rice wine or sherry
½ teaspoon cornstarch
½ teaspoon sesame oil
½ teaspoon sugar

1 Treat the beef according to "How to Tenderize
Meat" on page 13. This is an optional step.
2 Marinate the beef with all the Marinade ingredients, about 15 minutes.
3 Heat 1 tablespoon of the oil in a wok or skillet
over high heat. Stir-fry the beef until the beef
is browned on the outside but still pink inside.
Dish out and set aside.
4 Heat the remaining oil in a wok or skillet over high
heat. Stir-fry the garlic and the ginger until aromatic,
and then add the green bell pepper, red bell pepper,
onion, and black pepper. Stir-fry until you smell the
aroma from the ingredients in the wok.
5 Transfer the beef back into the wok or skillet. Stir-
fry until the beef is cooked through and the center of
the meat is no longer pink, about 1–2 minutes. Dish
out and serve immediately with steamed rice.

Black Pepper Beef Hei Jiao Niu Rou

I love the combination of bell pepper and black pepper in Chinese stir-
fries. These two ingredients, coupled with the right type of meat will
often guarantee a successful dish.

If you love the sweetness and slightly charred taste of caramelized
onions, stir-fry the onions and bell pepper slightly longer before adding
the beef to the stir-fry. You will be rewarded with a richer flavored Black
Pepper Beef.

Sweet-and-Sour Pork Gu Lao Rou

Sweet-and-Sour Pork, the ubiquitous and arguably one of the most well known Chinese pork dishes, is Cantonese in origin. The secret of an authentic Sweet-and-Sour Pork dish is in the perfect balance of the sweet versus sour flavor of the sauce. Mastering this recipe means making the best Sweet-and-Sour Sauce, which I reveal on page 30. Of course, nicely fried pork, along with fresh, and colorful ingredients, is equally important. Ultimately though, the Sweet-and-Sour Sauce is the heart and soul of this dish. I like my Sweet-and-Sour Pork just barely coated with the sauce, this way the pork pieces remain crispy. If you prefer the Americanized version with a heavier gravy, increase the portion of the Sweet-and-Sour Sauce to your liking.

Serves 4 as part of a multicourse meal

8 oz (250 g) pork tenderloin, pork butt,
   or pork neck
Oil, for deep-frying
2 tablespoons oil, for stir-frying
1 clove garlic, minced
½ small red bell pepper, deseeded and cut into
   pieces
½ small green bell pepper, deseeded and cut
   into pieces
½ small onion, quartered
1 slice canned pineapple ring, cut into pieces
2 green onions (scallions), white parts only,
   cut into 2 in (5 cm) lengths
½ cup (125 ml) Sweet-and-Sour Sauce (page 30)

Marinade
1 teaspoon soy sauce
1 teaspoon cornstarch
½ teaspoon Chinese rice wine or sherry

Frying Batter
½ cup (65 g) all-purpose flour, sifted
¼ cup (35 g) cornstarch
½ teaspoon baking soda
1 egg white
⅓ cup (80 ml) water
1 tablespoon oil
Pinch of salt

COOK'S NOTE: If you feel that the frying batter is too thick, add a little more water to it. To make the pork extra crispy, increase the temperature of the oil and deep-fry a second time. If you like more sauce, double the portion of the Sweet-and-Sour Sauce.

1 Cut the pork into bite-sized pieces and marinate with the Marinade ingredients for 15 minutes.

2 Mix all the ingredients in the Frying Batter until well combined. Add the marinated pork into the Frying Batter, stir to evenly coat with the batter.

3 Heat 2 to 3 inches (5 to 7.5 cm) of the oil in a wok or stockpot to 350°F (175°C) for deep-frying. Gently drop the pork into the oil and loosen them up immediately with the spatula to prevent the pork from clumping together.

4 Deep-fry them to a light golden brown or until the batter becomes crispy. Dish out with a strainer or slotted spoon, draining the excess oil by laying the pork on a dish lined with paper towels. Discard or reserve the oil for use in another recipe.

5 To stir-fry, heat 2 tablespoons of the oil in a wok or skillet over high heat. Add the garlic and stir-fry to a light brown before adding the peppers, onion, pineapple, and green onion. Stir the ingredients a few times and then add the Sweet-and-Sour Sauce.

6 As soon as the Sweet-and-Sour Sauce thickens, add the fried pork into the wok or skillet. Stir continuously until all the ingredients are well coated with the sauce. Dish out and serve immediately with steamed rice.

Cantonese BBQ Pork Char Siu

If you've been to any Chinatown, the sight of dangling roast meat (complete with pig's heads!) and Char Siu in the display window of Chinese BBQ restaurants can either tempt you or frighten you. Despite the unsightly exhibition at these traditional Chinese eateries, Cantonese BBQ Pork is savory, sticky sweet, and imbued with a unique oven-roasted aroma. My good friend Shirley taught me how to make this Cantonese BBQ Pork. Her recipe has been tried and tested many times and rivals the best that Chinatown has to offer. Give it a try and I am certain that you will agree.

Serves 4 as part of a multicourse meal

1 lb (500 g) pork butt or pork neck, cut into 4 pieces
3 cloves garlic, finely minced
1 tablespoon oil
½ cup (125 ml) Chinese BBQ Sauce (page 29)

1 Rub the garlic evenly on the pork pieces and marinate the pork with 2/3 of the Chinese BBQ Sauce overnight.

2 Add the oil into the remaining Chinese BBQ Sauce. Stir well and keep in the refrigerator.

3 The next day, preheat the oven to 375°F (190°C). Place the pork in a roasting pan.

Using a small brush, brush the pork with the barbecue sauce.

4 When the oven is heated, put the pork in the oven and roast for 15 minutes.

5 Turn the pork over and brush the pork surface with the sauce. Roast for another 15 minutes.

6 Brush the pork with the sauce for one last time before broiling on high heat until the pork is slightly charred on the surface, about 2–3 minutes. Repeat the same for the other side. Make sure not to burn the surface, check at the 2–minute mark. Take the pork out, let it cool, and then slice it into bite-sized pieces. Drizzle the remaining Chinese BBQ Sauce over the dish and serve immediately.

Pork Ribs with Black Beans

I am sure most people are familiar with the small tray of steamed spare ribs served at dim sum restaurants. This Pork Ribs with Black Beans is precisely the same, except here it is being served as an entrée instead of as dim sum. If you like spare ribs, this is an easy recipe that you can make quite effortlessly. I am particularly fond of the juice seeping out of the spare ribs after steaming. These ribs taste great when served with plain rice.

Serves 4 as part of a multicourse meal

12 oz (350 g) pork spare ribs, cut into 1½ in (3.75 cm) riblets
1 tablespoon Chinese rice wine or sherry
1 teaspoon cornstarch
2 teaspoons oil
3 cloves garlic, minced
1 tablespoon fermented black beans (douchi), rinsed and coarsely chopped
2 tablespoons chopped green onion (scallion)
2 teaspoons soy sauce
½ teaspoon chicken bouillon powder
½ teaspoon sugar
¼ teaspoon sesame oil
3 dashes white pepper
1 red finger-length chili, thinly sliced, to garnish

1 Treat the spare ribs according to "How to Tenderize Meat" on page 12. This is an optional step.
2 Marinate the spare ribs with the rice wine and cornstarch in a bowl, about 30 minutes.
3 Heat the oil in a wok or skillet over high heat. Add the garlic, fermented black beans, and 1 tablespoon of the green onion (scallion) and stir-fry until aromatic, about 1 minute. Dish out into a small bowl and add the soy sauce, chicken bouillon powder, sugar, sesame oil, and white pepper. Stir to combine well.
4 Transfer the spare ribs into a deep plate and pour the seasonings on top of the spare ribs and steam on high heat until the ribs are cooked, about 20 minutes.
5 Garnish with the sliced red chilies and the remaining 1 tablespoon of chopped green onion. Serve immediately with steamed rice.

1 Treat the beef according to "How to Tenderize Meat" on page 12. This is an optional step.
2 Marinate the beef with the ingredients for the Marinade, for about 15 minutes.
3 Bring the water to a boil and add a few drops of oil. Blanch the broccoli florets in the hot water, about 10 seconds. Remove the broccoli immediately with a strainer or slotted spoon, draining the excess water. Set aside.
4 Heat 1 tablespoon of the oil in a wok or skillet over high heat. Stir-fry the beef until the beef is browned on the outside but still pink inside. Dish out and set aside.
5 Combine all the Sauce ingredients in a bowl. Set aside.
6 Heat the remaining oil in a wok or skillet over high heat. Add the ginger and stir-fry until aromatic. Transfer the beef into the wok or skillet and stir-fry until the beef is cooked through and the center of the meat is no longer pink, about 1–2 minutes. Add the broccoli and then the Sauce, stir to combine the ingredients well.
7 As soon as the Sauce thickens, dish out and serve immediately with steamed rice.

Beef with Broccoli Xi Lan Hua Niu Rou

I think the United States grew up on Beef with Broccoli—the popular beef stir-fry dish is slathered in an all-too-familiar rich brown sauce. You could say that Beef with Broccoli is the poster child of American-Chinese food even though the traditional Chinese broccoli had been replaced with the more accessible and widely available "western" broccoli. I used to roll my eyes whenever I heard about Beef with Broccoli. However, I have to say that when it's cooked properly, that is, without dousing the beef in a thick goopy sauce and accompanied by overcooked broccoli, this dish can be great. The beef should be tender and succulent; the broccoli should be flash cooked, briefly blanched, and then lightly stir-fried with the beef; and the sauce should be lightly administered. If you have these three elements correctly cooked, you'll be serving an almost authentic version of Chinese Beef with Broccoli.

Serves 2 as a main dish with rice or 4 as part of
   a multicourse meal

8 oz (250 g) beef tenderloin, flank steak or
   flap meat, cut into pieces
Water, for boiling
6 oz (175 g) broccoli florets
2½ tablespoons oil
One 1 in (2.5 cm) piece fresh ginger, peeled
   and sliced into thin pieces

Marinade
½ tablespoon soy sauce
1 teaspoon Chinese rice wine or sherry
¼ teaspoon sesame oil
3 dashes white pepper
1 tablespoon cornstarch

Sauce
1 tablespoon soy sauce
1 tablespoon oyster sauce
¼ teaspoon sesame oil
½ teaspoon sugar
1 teaspoon cornstarch
4 tablespoons water

COOK'S NOTE: The typical Beef with Broccoli served in the Chinese restaurants in the United States are always drenched in a brown sauce, with overcooked broccoli. My version is not your typical Beef with Broccoli—it has less sauce and the broccoli is lightly cooked to ensure the best texture.

Chapter 5

Poultry

Of all the meats, I love chicken the most. Chicken is an essential part of my diet and, luckily for me, there's no shortage of chicken recipes in Chinese cuisine. Chicken is ideal for Chinese cooking because chicken meat's subtle flavor combines perfectly with the spices and seasonings typically found in Chinese cuisine.

Duck, on the other hand, is not as easy to prepare at home. However, in this chapter, you will find a simple Roast Duck (page 93) recipe that you can make rather painlessly at home (no air pump or compressor required!). In fact, the roast duck is so good that my hubby thought I got it from a Chinese restaurant!

Kung Pao Chicken　Gong Bao Ji Ding

Kung Pao Chicken is a classic dish in Sichuan cuisine. Originally from the Sichuan province in central western China, Kung Pao Chicken is probably more famous and popular outside of China than it is in its motherland. Despite my many travels to China, I had never had Kung Pao Chicken, not even once. I can only blame it on my numerous bad experiences with the westernized versions of Kung Pao Chicken; I simply had no desire to try an authentic version of the dish. When I went to Chengdu, the culinary capital of Sichuan in June 2008, I knew it was time to try the real Kung Pao Chicken and I'm glad I did. At a traditional Sichuan restaurant in a small alley beside a modern mall where the chef spoke only local Sichuan dialect, I had my first bite of authentic Kung Pao Chicken—explosively fiery, numbing, with a strong vinegary note. It was a sublime dining experience and the taste still lingers in my mouth.

Serves 2 as a main dish with rice or 4 as part of a multicourse meal

8 oz (250 g) skinless, boneless chicken breast, cut into bite-sized cubes
1 teaspoon Chinese rice wine or sherry
1 tablespoon cornstarch
2 tablespoons oil
1 tablespoon Sichuan Peppercorn Oil (page 27)
1 clove garlic, thinly sliced
One 1 in (2.5 cm) piece fresh ginger, peeled and sliced into thin pieces
10–15 dried red finger-length chilies, deseeded and cut into 2 in (5 cm) lengths
3 heaping tablespoons roasted peanuts
1 green onion (scallion), trimmed and cut into small rounds

Sauce
1½ tablespoon soy sauce
½ teaspoon dark soy sauce
1 teaspoon Chinese black vinegar
½ teaspoon Chinese rice wine or sherry
1 teaspoon sugar
3 dashes white pepper
2 tablespoons water
1 teaspoon cornstarch

1 Treat the chicken according to "How to Tenderize Meat" on page 12. This is an optional step.
2 Marinate the chicken with the rice wine or sherry and cornstarch for 10 minutes.
3 Mix all the ingredients for the Sauce in a small bowl. Set aside.
4 Heat ¹/₂ tablespoon of the oil in a wok or skillet over high heat and stir-fry the marinated chicken cubes until they are half-cooked or the surface turns opaque. Dish out and set aside.
5 Heat the remaining oil and the Sichuan Peppercorn Oil in the wok or skillet over high heat. Add the garlic and ginger, stir quickly with the spatula before adding the dried red chilies. Stir-fry until you smell the spicy aroma of the dried chilies.
6 Return the chicken to the wok or skillet and stir quickly with the spatula. Add the Sauce and stir continuously until the chicken meat is nicely coated with it.
7 Stir in the roasted peanuts and green onion, combining them thoroughly with the ingredients in the wok or skillet. Dish out and serve immediately with steamed rice.

Serves 2 as a main dish with rice or 4 as part of a
    multicourse meal

8 oz (250 g) skinless, boneless chicken breast or leg
    meat, cut into bite-sized cubes
1 wood ear mushroom
1 teaspoon Chinese rice wine or sherry
1 tablespoon cornstarch
3 tablespoons oil
3–4 cloves garlic, minced
½ small green bell pepper, deseeded and cut into
    pieces
½ small red bell pepper, deseeded and cut into pieces
2 oz (50 g) canned bamboo shoots, rinsed
1 green onion (scallion), trimmed and cut into 1 in
    (2.5 cm) lengths

Sauce
2 tablespoons soy sauce
¾ teaspoon dark soy sauce
1 tablespoon Chinese black vinegar
1 teaspoon store-bought chili oil or Homemade Chili
    Oil (page 27)
½ teaspoon sugar
1 heaping teaspoon cornstarch
3 tablespoons water
¼ teaspoon salt or to taste

1 Treat the chicken according to "How to Tenderize
Meat" on page 12. This is an optional step.
2 Soak the wood ear mushroom in warm water, about
15 minutes. Cut into pieces.
3 Marinate the chicken with the rice wine or sherry and
cornstarch for 10 minutes.
4 Mix all the ingredients for the Sauce in a small bowl.
Set aside.
5 Heat 1 tablespoon of the oil in a wok or skillet over high
heat. Add the chicken and stir-fry until half-cooked or the
surface turns opaque. Dish out and set aside.
6 Heat the remaining 2 tablespoons of oil in the wok
or skillet over high heat. Add the garlic and stir-fry
until aromatic, then add the wood ear mushroom, bell
peppers, and bamboo shoots. Stir-fry the ingredients
until you smell the peppery aroma from the bell peppers,
about 1 minute.
7 Return the chicken to the wok or skillet, stirring to
combine well with the ingredients. Pour in the Sauce and
stir continuously until the chicken meat is cooked and
well coated with the Sauce. Stir in the green onion, dish
out and serve immediately with steamed rice.

Chicken with Garlic Sauce

I adore garlic and use it copiously in my Chinese stir-fries. While I
can't deny its medicinal properties, it's the zealous aroma that mat-
ters most to me. Chicken with Garlic Sauce is one such dish where I
use lots of garlic in the stir-fry as the different ingredients such as
bamboo shoots, wood ear mushrooms, and bell peppers readily soak
up the garlicky flavor of the sauce.

On the other hand, the Chinese black vinegar lends the sharp flavor
so the end result is a great chicken dish that is aromatic, appetizing,
and remarkably tasty. If you like your food garlicky, you can add
more to your preference.

Black Bean Sauce Chicken

When I was pursuing my Masters Degree in the Midwest, Black Bean Sauce Chicken was my absolutely favorite comfort dish to prepare. It was also one of the most requested meals during weekend potluck parties. My Venezuelan friends loved this dish so much that they created a nickname for it: *Chicken with Chinese Flies* ("flies" because of the black color and somewhat fly-*ish* appearance of Chinese fermented black beans). They would pick the preserved black beans out, savoring each one of them. Chinese fermented black bean or *douchi* is a versatile ingredient that goes well with meat or seafood. The taste of the beans is bold, sharp, and salty with a pungent, yeasty note. Instant black bean paste made of fermented black beans, garlic, and other seasonings are commercially available, but nothing beats the original *douchi* for authentic flavor.

Serves 2 as a main dish with rice or 4 as part of a multicourse meal

8 oz (250 g) skinless, boneless chicken breast, cut into bite-sized cubes
1 tablespoon Chinese rice wine or sherry
1 teaspoon cornstarch
2½ tablespoons oil
One 1 in (2.5 cm) piece fresh ginger, peeled and sliced into thin pieces
3 cloves garlic, finely minced
2 tablespoons fermented black beans (douchi), rinsed and coarsely chopped
½ small green bell pepper, deseeded and cut into pieces
½ small red bell pepper, deseeded and cut into pieces
1 red finger-length chili, deseeded and cut into pieces
½ small onion, quartered
Salt to taste

Sauce
2 teaspoons soy sauce
1 tablespoon sugar
¼ teaspoon sesame oil
3 dashes white pepper
2 tablespoons water
1 teaspoon cornstarch

1 Treat the chicken according to "How to Tenderize Meat" on Page 12. This is an optional step.
2 Marinate the chicken with the rice wine or sherry and cornstarch. Set aside for 10 minutes.
3 Mix all the ingredients for the Sauce in a small bowl. Set aside.
4 Heat ½ tablespoon of the oil in a wok or skillet over high heat. Add the chicken and stir-fry until half-cooked or the surface turns opaque. Dish out and set aside
5 Heat the remaining 2 tablespoons of the oil in a wok or skillet over high heat. Add the ginger and garlic, stir-fry until they turn light brown. Stir in the fermented black beans, bell peppers, red chili, and onion. Stir-fry until aromatic, about 1–2 minutes.
6 Return the chicken to the wok or skillet, stir and blend well with all the ingredients in the wok, about 1 minute. Add the Sauce and continue stirring until the chicken is cooked through. Add salt to taste. Dish out and serve immediately with steamed rice.

Sichuan Spicy Chicken La Zi Ji

I first encountered Sichuan Spicy Chicken, or *Chongqing La Zi Ji*, at a Sichuan restaurant in China. At the restaurant, almost every table had a serving of a chicken dish buried under a mountain heap of dried red chilies. I tried the dish and was instantly hooked on the aromatic, fiery, numbing, and deeply flavorful chicken. It was delicious! According to my local friend, Sichuan Spicy Chicken was invented some 14 years ago in a small restaurant outside of Chongqing, the capital of Sichuan, in the town of Ge Le Shan and has since become a popular dish. My friend Chef Wang taught me this recipe and I have toned it down significantly to suit your palate.

Serves 4 as part of a multicourse meal

10 oz (330 g) skinless, boneless chicken meat (breasts, thighs, or legs), cut into bite-sized cubes
½ tablespoon Chinese rice wine or sherry
2 tablespoons cornstarch
½ teaspoon salt
Oil, for deep-frying
1 tablespoon store-bought chili oil or Homemade Chili Oil (page 27)
1 tablespoon Sichuan Peppercorn Oil (page 27)
3 cloves garlic, thinly sliced
20 dried red finger-length chilies, deseeded and cut into 2 in (5 cm) lengths
½ teaspoon chicken bouillon powder
¼ teaspoon sugar
Salt to taste
3 green onions (scallions), white parts only, trimmed and cut into small rounds

1 Marinate the chicken with the Chinese rice wine, cornstarch, and salt, about 15 minutes.
2 Heat 2 to 3 inches (5 to 7.5 cm) of the oil in a wok or stockpot to 350°F (175°C) for deep-frying. Gently drop the chicken into the oil and loosen them up immediately with the spatula to prevent the chicken from clumping together.
3 Deep-fry the chicken to a light golden brown. Dish out with a strainer or slotted spoon, draining the excess oil by laying the chicken on a dish lined with paper towels. Discard or reserve the oil for use in other recipe.
4 To stir-fry, heat the chili oil and Sichuan Peppercorn Oil in a wok or skillet over high heat. Add the garlic, stir quickly with the spatula before adding the dried red chilies. Stir-fry until you smell the spicy aroma of the dried chilies.
5 Return the chicken to the wok or skillet and add the chicken bouillon powder, sugar, salt, and green onions. Stir quickly with the spatula to combine all the ingredients in the wok or skillet. Dish out and serve immediately with steamed rice.

> **COOK'S NOTE:** Sichuan Spicy Chicken is supposed to be laden with lots of dried red chilies and explosively spicy. Reduce (or increase) the amount of chilies used to fit your tolerance for heat.

Orange Chicken Chen Pi Ji

Orange Chicken (also known as orange peel chicken or tangerine chicken) derives its name from the use of dried orange peel in the traditional recipe. Unfortunately, like many Chinese dishes, the Orange Chicken served in the United States often looks like a gloppy mess. When I was developing this recipe, I was determined to do it right and do justice to this dish. The end result is not your typical Chinese takeout equivalent, but an appetizing, refined, and robust rendition—with just the right hint of heat from the dried red chilies. The orange peel—a hard-to-find ingredient in regular markets—has been replaced with fresh orange juice for a subtle zing.

Serves 2 as a main dish with rice or 4 as part of a multicourse meal

8 oz (250 g) skinless, boneless chicken meat (breasts, thighs, or legs), cut into slices or cubes
2 tablespoons cornstarch
Oil, for deep-frying
1 tablespoon oil
2 cloves garlic, minced
5 dried red finger-length chilies
2 green onions (scallions), white parts only, trimmed and cut into 1 in (2.5 cm) lengths

Sauce
3 tablespoons fresh orange juice
2 tablespoons soy sauce
1 teaspoon Chinese rice wine or sherry
1 teaspoon Chinese rice vinegar
¼ teaspoon sesame oil
2½ tablespoons sugar
1 teaspoon cornstarch
1 tablespoon water

1 Mix all the ingredients for the Sauce in a small bowl. Toss the chicken with the cornstarch in a separate bowl. Set aside.
2 Heat 2 to 3 inches (5 to 7.5 cm) of the oil in a wok or stockpot to 350°F (175°C) for deep-frying. Gently drop the chicken into the oil and loosen them up immediately with the spatula to prevent the chicken from clumping together.
3 Deep-fry the chicken to a light golden brown. Dish out with a strainer or slotted spoon, draining the excess oil by laying the chicken on a dish lined with paper towels. Discard or reserve the oil for use in another recipe.
4 Heat 1 tablespoon of oil in a wok or skillet over high heat. Add the garlic, stir quickly with the spatula before adding the dried red chilies. Stir-fry until you smell the spicy aroma of the dried chilies.
5 Return the chicken to the wok or skillet and add the Sauce. Stir continuously until the chicken is well coated with the Sauce. Stir in the green onions, dish out and serve immediately with steamed rice.

> **COOK'S NOTE:** If you like your Orange Chicken with more sauce, double the portion of the Sauce.

Cashew Chicken Yao Guo Ji Ding

Cashew Chicken was one of my favorite childhood dishes because of my love for cashew nuts. Growing up, I didn't like chicken that much so I would pick out all the cashew nuts in the dish and eat them with my rice. As the years have passed I have formed a strong affinity for chicken, especially the tender, silky, velvety chicken meat served at Chinese restaurants. Somehow, home-cooked chicken just couldn't compare, the texture was never as smooth as the ones served at restaurants. I resolved to unlock the secret technique used at Chinese restaurants and the answer is baking soda. You can learn all about it on page 12, "How to Tenderize Meat."

Serves 2 as a main dish with rice or 4 as part of a multicourse meal

10 oz (330 g) skinless, boneless chicken breast, cut into 1 in (2.5 cm) cubes
1 teaspoon Chinese rice wine or sherry
1 tablespoon cornstarch
2 tablespoons oil
One 1 in (2.5 cm) piece fresh ginger, peeled and sliced
½ small green bell pepper, cut into pieces
½ small red bell pepper, cut into pieces
½ cup (75 g) roasted cashew nuts
¼ teaspoon salt or to taste

Sauce
½ teaspoon Chinese rice wine or sherry
½ tablespoon oyster sauce
¼ teaspoon sesame oil
1 teaspoon soy sauce
½ teaspoon sugar
3 tablespoons water
1 teaspoon cornstarch
3 dashes white pepper

1 Treat the chicken according to "How to Tenderize Meat" on Page 12. This is an optional step.
2 Marinate the chicken with the rice wine or sherry and cornstarch for 10 minutes.
3 Mix all the ingredients for the Sauce in a small bowl. Set aside.
4 Heat ¹/₂ tablespoon of the oil in a wok or skillet over high heat. Add the chicken and stir-fry until half-cooked or the surface turns opaque. Dish out and set aside.
5 Heat the remaining oil in the wok or skillet over high heat. When the oil starts to smoke, add in the ginger, green and red bell peppers.
6 Stir-fry the ingredients until you smell the peppery aroma from the bell peppers, and then add the chicken back into the wok or skillet. Pour in the Sauce and stir continuously until the chicken meat is cooked and well coated with the Sauce.
7 Add the cashew nuts and do a few quick stirs. Add the salt to taste and stir to blend well. Dish out and serve immediately with steamed rice.

> **COOK'S NOTE:** If you like your Cashew Chicken with more sauce, double the portion of the Sauce.

Lemon Chicken   Ning Meng Ji

Lemon is not a commonly used ingredient in Chinese cuisine. In fact, Lemon Chicken is probably one of the few dishes that does take advantage of the citrusy tang of lemon. Whenever I need something to stimulate my appetite, I make this dish because it's so inviting and palatable.

It's best to use a skinless, boneless chicken meat when preparing Lemon Chicken. After deep-frying the chicken with a crispy and crumbly batter, the chicken will be cut into pieces before the lemon sauce is poured on top of it.

Serves 2–3 as part of a multicourse meal

12 oz (350 g) skinless, boneless chicken breast
1 large egg, beaten
Oil, for deep-frying

Marinade
1½ teaspoons soy sauce
½ teaspoon sesame oil
1 tablespoon cornstarch
1 teaspoon Chinese rice wine or sherry

Sauce
3 tablespoons fresh lemon juice
2 tablespoons plum sauce
2 teaspoons sugar
4 tablespoons water
½ teaspoon cornstarch
A pinch of salt, or to taste

Coating
¼ cup (35 g) all-purpose flour
¼ cup (35 g) cornstarch
1 teaspoon baking soda

1 Cut the chicken breast into two equal-sized pieces and marinate with all the ingredients for Marinade for 30 minutes.
2 Mix and then sift all the ingredients for the Coating. Set aside.
3 Mix all the ingredients for the Sauce in a saucepan. Heat the saucepan over medium to low heat. Stir the Sauce to blend well. Once the Sauce starts to bubble and boil, remove the saucepan from the heat.
4 Dip the chicken in the egg, and then dust with the Coating evenly. Shake off the excess Coating.
5 Heat 2 to 3 inches (5 to 7.5 cm) of the oil in a wok or stockpot to 350°F (175°C) for deep-frying. Gently drop the chicken into the oil.
6 Deep-fry the chicken to a light golden brown. Dish out with a strainer or slotted spoon, draining the excess oil by laying the chicken on a dish lined with paper towels. Discard or reserve the oil for use in another recipe.
7 Cut the chicken into pieces. Drizzle the Sauce on top and serve immediately with steamed rice.

COOK'S NOTE: If you like your Lemon Chicken with more sauce, increase the portion of the Sauce to your liking.

Roast Duck Kao Ya

At first I was intimidated by the work involved in making a Roast Duck. I have watched way too many Chinese cookery programs and read numerous articles about the Chinese way of roasting duck (using an air compressor, bicycle pump, S-shape metal hooks, and so on). I don't have an Iron Chef kitchen stadium at home, and I just don't have half the tools needed to make a Chinatown-worthy roast duck. So I improvised my own Roast Duck recipe so every home cook can feel comfortable making this sumptuous dish at home. I am not really a duck person and I have to say that I might even begin to love duck after tasting how great this came out. My hubby was so impressed with my work that he gave me two thumbs up!

One 2 in (5 cm) piece fresh ginger, peeled and pounded
2 green onions (scallions), trimmed and cut into 2 in (5 cm) lengths
Water, for boiling
2 duck leg quarters, about 1 lb (500 g)
3 tablespoons hoisin sauce

Marinade
½ teaspoon Chinese five spice powder
1 teaspoon honey
½ teaspoon salt
2 tablespoons soy sauce
3 dashes white pepper

1 Add the ginger and one of the green onions to the water and bring it to boil. Add the duck and boil until the duck is half-cooked, about 3 minutes. Transfer the duck out and let it cool at room temperature.
2 Mix all the ingredients for the Marinade in a small bowl and rub it on the duck generously. Transfer the duck and the remaining Marinade to a resealable plastic bag and marinate overnight. Make sure the duck is well coated with the Marinade.
3 The next day, take the duck out from the fridge. Place the duck on a wire rack and air dry for 3 hours. Start with the skin side up and then turn it over to air dry the bottom part of the leg quarters. Make sure that the skin is completely dry. Use a fan to help the air-drying process, if desired.
4 Preheat the oven to 475°F (245°C). Arrange the duck on an aluminum foil in a roasting pan. Roast for 15 minutes, with the skin side up. Transfer the duck out at the 15 minutes mark, brush the duck skin with the duck oil that seeps out during the roasting process. Lower the heat to 375°F (190°C) and roast for another 30–40 minutes, or until the skin turns brown and crispy. Check at 30 minutes mark.
5 Transfer the duck out, let cool for 5–10 minutes, chop it up into pieces, and serve immediately with some of the green onion and hoisin sauce.

COOK'S NOTE: The duck leg quarters should submerge in the water during the boiling process.

Chapter 6

Seafood

Chinese are obsessed with seafood and I am
no exception. Growing up on an island, with my
late mother hailing from a fishing village, my
love affair with seafood started when I was little.
Every day, my mother would prepare at least
one seafood dish for my family—fish or shrimp
or both. Sometimes, we would get clams, squid,
or even crab. We were really spoiled.

If you've been to a seafood market in Asia,
for example: Sai Kung in Hong Kong, you will
know that the Chinese take their seafood
seriously—all sorts of live sea creatures are
swimming in the fish tanks and bins of edible
marine creatures are on display available as a
potential meal for enthusiastic diners.

Seafood is revered for its sweet, briny taste,
and highly prized for its texture and nutritional
values. Here, I share with you the ultimate
Chinese seafood recipes for your eating pleasure.

Shrimp with Snow Peas

Every spring, when fresh snow peas first hit my local farmer's market, I buy a bunch of them so I can prepare Shrimp with Snow Peas—one of the best Chinese stir-fry recipes for snow peas. The vibrant green color and delicate taste of snow peas match perfectly with the shrimp, just the sight of this dish always sparks a healthy appetite. When making this dish, it's important to not overcook the snow peas. They should be blanched quickly and then stir-fried with the shrimp.

Serves 4 as part of a multicourse meal

8 oz (250 g) shelled and deveined medium-sized raw shrimp
Water, for boiling
2 oz (50 g) snow peas, tips and strings removed
½ small carrot, sliced into pieces
2 tablespoons oil
One 1 in (2.5 cm) piece fresh ginger, peeled and sliced into thin pieces

Sauce
1 teaspoon Chinese rice wine or sherry
¼ teaspoon cornstarch
½ tablespoon oyster sauce
¼ teaspoon salt
¼ teaspoon sesame oil
½ teaspoon sugar
4 tablespoons water
3 dashes white pepper

1 Treat the shrimp according to "How to Make Shrimp Bouncy" on page 13. This is an optional step.
2 Mix all the ingredients for the Sauce in a small bowl. Set aside.
3 Bring the water to a boil in a medium saucepan and add a few drops of oil. Blanch the snow peas and the carrot in the hot water, about 10 seconds. Remove the snow peas and carrot immediately with a strainer or slotted spoon, draining the excess water. Set aside.
4 Heat 1 tablespoon of the oil in a wok or skillet over high heat. Stir-fry the shrimp until half-cooked or the surface turns opaque. Dish out and set aside.
5 Heat the remaining oil in a wok or skillet over high heat. Add the ginger and stir-fry until aromatic. Transfer the shrimp, snow peas, carrot, and the Sauce into the wok or skillet and stir-fry until the shrimp is cooked, about 1 minute. Dish out and serve immediately with steamed rice.

Sauteed Scallops with Asparagus

When it comes to scallops, I much prefer scallops stir-fried in a light sauce as opposed to a stronger sauce (black bean sauce), which I find overwhelms the flavor of the scallops. So this recipe is purely my personal preference: I want the natural, mild, and delicate taste of scallops to shine through. In this recipe, the white sauce does not camouflage the sweet flavor of the scallops, in fact, it highlights them so well that every bite is memorable.

Serves 4 as part of a multicourse meal

Water, for boiling
12 oz (350 g) fresh scallops
4 oz (100 g) asparagus
2 tablespoons oil
One 1 in (2.5 cm) piece fresh ginger, peeled
 and sliced into thin pieces
6 fresh or canned button mushrooms, sliced
½ small carrot, sliced into pieces
2 green onions (scallions), white parts only,
 trimmed and cut into 1 in (2.5 cm) lengths

Sauce
1 teaspoon Chinese rice wine or sherry
1 heaping teaspoon cornstarch
1 teaspoon fish sauce
¼ teaspoon salt
¼ teaspoon sesame oil
½ teaspoon sugar
4 tablespoons water
3 dashes white pepper

1 Bring the water to boil and blanch the scallops until they are half-cooked, about 30–45 seconds, depending on the size of the scallops.
2 Remove the scallops with a strainer or slotted spoon, draining the excess water. Set aside.
3 Mix all the ingredients for the Sauce in a small bowl. Set aside.
4 Trim about 1 inch (2.5 cm) off the bottom end of each asparagus stalk and cut the asparagus into 1¹/₂-inch (3.75 cm) lengths.
5 Heat the oil in a wok or skillet over high heat. Stir-fry the ginger until aromatic. Transfer the scallops, asparagus, button mushrooms, and carrot into the wok or skillet and then stir-fry for about 1 minute.
6 Pour in the Sauce and stir continuously until it thickens and all the ingredients are well coated with the Sauce. Stir in the green onion, dish out and serve immediately with steamed rice.

Black Bean Sauce Clams

Serves 4 as part of a multicourse meal

Out of all the marine bivalves, my favorite is the clam. Back in Malaysia, in my hometown of Penang, there are many beaches with an abundant supply of clams. During my most recent visit, my family and I chartered a boat to an offshore island where local fishermen congregate for their daily catch. In no time, we filled our buckets with heaps of clams. We went home, cleaned the clams and shared our harvest with friends and family. We made Black Bean Sauce Clams, a favorite Chinese clam recipe, and served it with steamed white rice. The clams were briny, fresh, juicy, and delicious, especially with a bottle of cold beer.

2 tablespoons oil
1 clove garlic, minced
One 1 in (2.5 cm) piece fresh ginger, peeled and minced
1 tablespoon preserved black beans, rinsed and finely chopped
1½ lbs (750 g) Manila or little neck clams, scrubbed and rinsed
1 red finger-length chili, deseeded and sliced
Salt to taste
2 green onions (scallions), trimmed and cut into 2 in (5 cm) lengths

Sauce
¼ teaspoon dark soy sauce
1 teaspoon Chinese rice wine or sherry
¼ teaspoon sesame oil
2 teaspoons sugar
3 tablespoons water
3 dashes white pepper

1 Mix all the ingredients for the Sauce in a small bowl. Set aside.
2 Heat the oil in a wok or skillet over high heat. Stir-fry the minced garlic and ginger until aromatic, then add the preserved black beans and red chili, stir continuously until you smell the aroma of the preserved black beans, about 30 seconds.
3 Add the clams and then stir-fry for about 1 minute. Cover the wok or skillet with its lid until the clams open, about 2–3 minutes.
4 Remove the lid and add the Sauce. Stir until the clams are nicely coated with the Sauce. Add the salt, to taste.
5 Add the green onion and toss well with the clams. Dish out and serve immediately with steamed rice.

Serves 4 as part of a multicourse meal

8 oz (250 g) shelled and deveined medium-sized raw shrimp
1 tablespoon egg white
¼ teaspoon salt
½ cup (70 g) cornstarch
Oil, for frying

Dressing
½ tablespoon condensed milk
½ tablespoon honey
1 teaspoon fresh lemon juice
3 tablespoons mayonnaise

Walnut Glaze
½ cup (50 g) walnut halves
¼ cup (65 ml) water
¼ cup (50 g) sugar

1 Pat dry the shrimp with paper towels and marinate the shrimp with the egg white and salt, about 30 minutes.

2 To make the Walnut Glaze, rinse the walnut halves with cold water, drain, and set aside. Bring the water to a boil and add in the sugar. Keep stirring until the glaze thickens. Lower the heat to medium and add the walnut halves. Keep stirring until the mixture becomes golden brown or caramel in color. Transfer the walnut halves onto a parchment paper or wax paper to dry. (Regular paper will not work because the walnut will stick to it).

3 Mix all the ingredients for the Dressing in a bowl. Set aside.

4 Dust the marinated shrimp with the cornstarch evenly. Shake off the excess.

5 Heat 2 to 3 inches (5 to 7.5 cm) of the oil in a wok or stockpot to 350°F (175°C) for deep-frying. Gently drop the shrimp into the oil.

6 Deep-fry the shrimp to a light brown. Dish out with a strainer or slotted spoon, draining the excess oil by laying the shrimp on a dish lined with paper towels. Discard or reserve the oil for use in another recipe.

7 Combine the shrimp with the Dressing and toss well. Transfer the shrimp to a serving plate and garnish with glazed walnuts on top of the shrimp. Serve immediately with steamed rice.

Honey Walnut Shrimp   Mi Tao Xia

A junior co-worker once begged me for my Honey Walnut Shrimp recipe. He had spent a fortune splurging on this decadent dish at a posh Chinese restaurant, which was hurting his budget. It's hard not to love Honey Walnut Shrimp—deep-fried succulent shrimp, lightly coated with a creamy mayonnaise-based sauce, flecked with crunchy amber-colored glazed walnuts. With such mouthwatering ingredients, Honey Walnut Shrimp has become one of the most loved of the Chinese shrimp dishes.

Succulent Steamed Fish Fillets

The Chinese love steamed fish, especially steamed whole fish with its head and tail intact. I love steamed fish in its full body glory, but sometimes I find it a hassle to serve at home. First of all, it's not easy to find a live or fresh enough fish for steaming. Secondly, for a truly awesome Cantonese-style steamed fish, only certain fish are suitable—for example: rock cod and grouper, which are hard to find even though I live close to many Asian markets.

As a result, I started making steamed fish using fillet, which works exceedingly well and I can have it as often as I want. I like using red snapper, cod, or sea bass fillet for this dish. If you can't find these fish at your market, you can try the recipe with a mild-flavor fish such as flounder or sole.

Serves 4 as part of a multicourse meal

1½ lbs (750 g) fish fillet, about 1 in (2.5 cm) thick
One 2 in (5 cm) piece fresh ginger, peeled and sliced into thin pieces
1 tablespoon Chinese rice wine or sherry
½ teaspoon sesame oil
1 recipe Cantonese-style Steamed Fish Sauce (page 28)
1 green onion (scallion), trimmed and cut into thin threads, to garnish
2 tablespoons fresh coriander leaves (cilantro), to garnish

1 Arrange the fish fillet in a deep serving plate. (Depending on the fish you get, you might cut the fish fillet into a couple of equal-size pieces.) Add the ginger, rice wine or sherry, and sesame oil on top of the fish. Steam the fish for 5 minutes or until cooked.
2 Discard the ginger and completely remove the cloudy liquid seeping out from the fish.
3 Garnish the fish with green onion and coriander leaves. Pour the Cantonese-style Steamed Fish Sauce onto the fish and serve immediately with steamed rice.

> **COOK'S NOTE:** I like mild-flavored fish such as red snapper, cod, or sea bass for this recipe.

Clams with Ginger and Green Onions

The first Cantonese dish that I had ever prepared was Ginger and Green Onion Chicken, using a cookbook pamphlet that came with a bottle of oyster sauce. Ginger and green onion (scallion) are two of the most fundamental ingredients in Cantonese cooking—if you love Chinese cuisine you'll want to master the art of wok cooking these two items. I am a huge fan of the explosively flavorful ginger and green onion stir-fries: chicken, beef, crab, lobster, and in this case, clams. The spicy kick of the ginger, the oniony balance of the green onion, and the simple oyster sauce mixture turn the clams into a deeply flavorful dish.

Serves 4 as part of a multicourse meal

2 tablespoons oil
3 green onions (scallions), trimmed and
   cut into 2 in (5 cm) lengths
1½ lbs (750 g) Manila or little neck clams,
   scrubbed and rinsed
One 2 in (5 cm) piece fresh ginger, peeled
   and sliced into thin pieces

Sauce
¼ teaspoon dark soy sauce
1 teaspoon Chinese rice wine or sherry
1 tablespoon cornstarch
1 tablespoon oyster sauce
½ teaspoon sesame oil
Scant ½ tablespoon sugar
½ cup (125 ml) water
3 dashes white pepper

1 Mix all the ingredients for the Sauce in a small bowl. Set aside
2 Heat the oil in a wok or skillet over high heat. Stir-fry the ginger until aromatic. Add the clams and then stir-fry for about 1 minute.
3 Cover the wok or skillet with its lid until the clams open, about 2–3 minutes.
4 Remove the lid and lower the heat to medium. Add the Sauce and stir continuously until the clams are nicely coated with the Sauce.
5 Add the green onions and toss well with the clams. Dish out and serve immediately with steamed rice.

Sweet-and-Sour Fish

Much like its cousin, Sweet-and-Sour Pork (page 80), Sweet-and-Sour Fish is accented with layers of flavor: sweet, sour, salty, and savory. While the sauce base is the same (using Sweet-and-Sour Sauce, page 30), the accompanying ingredients are different. My good friend, Chef Robert Danhi, gave me the batter recipe used in this dish. Using only a mixture of egg whites and cornstarch, the fish fillet is coated with a thin layer of velvety batter, which offers a light, airy and crispy texture, absolutely ideal for the fish.

Serves 2 as a main dish with rice or 4 as part of a multicourse meal

8 oz (250 g) mild-flavor fish fillet, about 1 in (2.5 cm) thick, cut into bite-sized pieces
1 recipe Sweet-and-Sour Sauce (page 30)
Oil, for deep-frying
2 tablespoons oil
1 clove garlic, thinly sliced
One 1 in (2.5 cm) piece fresh ginger, peeled and sliced into thin pieces
½ small tomato, cut into wedges
½ small cucumber, cut into small pieces
½ small red or green bell pepper, deseeded and cut into pieces
1 green onion (scallion), trimmed and cut into 2 in (5 cm) lengths

Frying Batter
2 egg whites, beaten
¼ cup (35 g) cornstarch
¼ teaspoon salt

1 To make the Frying Batter, beat the egg white for 1 minute and then add the cornstarch and salt. Mix until it forms a smooth batter.

2 Add the fish fillet into the Frying Batter, stir to coat evenly with the batter.

3 Heat 2 to 3 inches (5 to 7.5 cm) of the oil in a wok or stockpot to 350°F (175°C) for deep-frying. Gently drop the fish into the oil and loosen them up immediately with the spatula to prevent the fish from clumping together.

4 Deep-fry the fish to a light golden brown. Dish out with a strainer or slotted spoon, draining the excess oil by laying the fish on a dish lined with paper towels. Discard or reserve the oil for use in another recipe.

5 Heat 2 tablespoons of the oil in a wok or skillet over high heat. Add the garlic and ginger and stir-fry to a light brown before adding the tomato, cucumber, and pepper. Stir the ingredients a few times and then add the Sweet-and-Sour Sauce.

6 As soon as the Sweet-and-Sour Sauce thickens, add the fish fillet and green onion into the wok or skillet. Stir continuously until all the ingredients are well coated with the sauce. Dish out and serve immediately with steamed rice.

> **COOK'S NOTE:** A mild flavor fish such as sole, cod, snapper, grouper, or halibut is great for this recipe. If you are not experienced with stir-frying fish fillet, get a firmer textured fish like the monkfish.

Oysters Steamed in the Half-Shell

When we lived in San Francisco, every weekend, my hubby and I would frequent a mom-and-pop Chinese restaurant called The Eight Immortals on Taravel Street, which offers some of the most delicious Cantonese food at a very decent price. Whenever we dined in, the Steamed Oyster in the Half-Shell was the one dish I would always order—big, fat, luxuriously smooth oysters on the half shell steamed with ginger, green onion, and bathed in a savory soy sauce.

Now that we live in Southern California, I only wished that Chinese restaurants here in the Greater Los Angeles area would offer steamed oysters on their menu. After searching high and low for it, I have finally given up. This is my homemade version, using the Cantonese-Style Steamed Fish Sauce from page 28.

Serves 4 as part of a multicourse meal

8 big fresh oysters in shell
1 recipe Cantonese-Style Steamed Fish Sauce
(page 28)
One 2 in (5 cm) piece fresh ginger, peeled and cut
into thin matchstick strips
1 green onion (scallion), cut into thin threads
2 tablespoons coriander leaves (cilantro)

1 Shuck the oysters with an oyster knife. Arrange the oyster in a deep serving plate and steam for 5 minutes or until cooked.
2 Remove the cloudy liquid seeping out from the oysters. Garnish the oysters with the ginger, green onion, and coriander leaves. Add some Cantonese-style Steamed Fish Sauce onto the oysters and serve immediately with steamed rice.

Chapter 7

Vegetables, Tofu and Eggs

A balanced multicourse Chinese meal often comes with a vegetable, egg, or tofu dish. In the rural areas of China, where vegetables are mostly homegrown, a humble lunch or dinner comes with at least two or three vegetable dishes—crisp and tender Chinese greens, beans, peas, and/or eggplants.

Egg and tofu dishes are also highly favored by the Chinese people because they are healthy and full of nutrients. Dishes such as Tea Leaf Eggs (page 107) are sold by street vendors or prepared at home, as a light snack throughout the day, while Mapo Tofu (page 109) is another favorite for many people.

Fish Fragrant Eggplant

I wasn't always a fan of eggplant, mostly because I'd never had an eggplant dish that wasn't overcooked. The ones I've had are always mushy, squishy, and the vibrant purple color skin had turned to an unsightly brown. I have been hestiant to eat eggplant based on those bad experiences. My negative stereotypes about eggplant completely changed when I tried this Sichuan eggplant prepared by my friend—the eggplant retains the enticing purple color, the core is spongy and absorbs the piquant flavors of the fish fragrant sauce. Eggplant is indeed delightful, if you know how to prepare it. My friend gave me this recipe and I have been cooking it at home since. This classic Sichuan recipe is a keeper. This is sometimes called "Fish Fragant" Eggplant.

> **COOK'S NOTE:** The name "fish fragrant" might be confusing to many because there isn't any fish in this recipe. Tale has it that this recipe originated from a Sichuan family who loved to eat fish. The wife used a combination of Chinese black vinegar, soy sauce, garlic, and ginger to cook fish. One day, she used the leftover "Fish Fragrant" sauce to make a non-fish dish and the family loved it. Since then, "Fish Fragrant" style of cooking has been adapted to a variety of dishes such as eggplant and pork.

Serves 4 as part of a multicourse meal

8 oz (250 g) Chinese or American eggplant, cut into 2 in (5 cm) length by ½ in (1.25 cm) thick
Oil, for deep-frying
1 tablespoon oil
2 cloves garlic, minced
One ½ in (1.25 cm) piece fresh ginger, peeled and minced
½ red finger-length chili, deseeded and cut into small pieces
1 heaping tablespoon chopped green onion (scallion)

Sauce
1½ tablespoons hot bean sauce
1 teaspoon soy sauce
¼ teaspoon dark soy sauce
1 tablespoon Chinese black vinegar
½ teaspoon sugar
2 tablespoons water
½ teaspoon cornstarch

Tea Leaf Eggs Cha Ye Dan

I am a huge fan of Chinese Tea Leaf Eggs because they are not only a wonderful treat but also make for real eye-candy. The marbled-effect on the eggs is achieved by gently cracking the eggs before steeping them in the tea mixture for hours, or even days. As the gorgeous marbled patterns start to form, the flavors of the tea and spices used in the recipe penetrate deeply into the eggs, creating the unmistakable aroma and fragrance of Chinese Tea Leaf Eggs. These eggs are great as an appetizer or a light snack between meals.

1 Mix all the ingredients in the Sauce in a small bowl. Set aside.
2 Cut the eggplant and soak the pieces immediately in cold water. Add some salt to the water to prevent the eggplant from turning brown. Pat dry with paper towels before deep-frying.
3 Heat 2 to 3 inches (5 to 7.5 cm) of the oil in a wok or skillet to 350°F (175°C) for deep-frying. Gently drop the eggplant into the oil and deep-fry for 10 seconds. Remove them with a strainer or slotted spoon, draining the excess oil by laying the eggplant on a dish lined with paper towels. Discard or reserve the oil for another recipe.
4 Heat 1 tablespoon of oil in a wok or skillet over high heat. Add the garlic and ginger and stir-fry to a light brown. Add the red chilies and and then stir-in the Sauce. As soon as the Sauce thickens, put in the eggplant and green onion. Stir continuously until the eggplant is well coated with the Sauce. Dish out and serve immediately with steamed rice.

Makes 12 eggs or serves 6 as an
  appetizer

4 cups (1 liter) water
12 large eggs

Tea Mixture
4 cups (1 liter) water
**3 heaping tablespoons Chinese puer
  tea leaf or black tea**
1 cinnamon stick
3 star anise
6 tablespoons soy sauce
3 teaspoons dark soy sauce
1 teaspoon Chinese five spice powder
1 teaspoon sugar
1 teaspoon salt

1 Add 4 cups (1 liter) of water to a pot and gently drop in the eggs. Make sure the water covers the eggs. Bring the water to boil over high heat. Boil until the eggs are cooked, about 10 minutes.
2 Remove the hard-boiled eggs from the boiling water and rinse them with cold running water. Using the back of a teaspoon, gently tap the eggshell to crack the shell. Discard the water in the pot.
3 To make the Tea Mixture, heat the water in a pot and bring it to a boil. Add the rest of the ingredients and return to a boil.
4 Transfer the eggs to the pot and boil the eggs with the Tea Mixture for 10 minutes. Reduce the heat to low. Simmer the eggs for at least 2 hours.
5 Serve the eggs immediately or leave them in the Tea Mixture overnight to further develop the color and flavor. Tea Leaf Eggs are best served the next day.

Scrambled Eggs with Shrimp

Scrambled Eggs with Shrimp is prized for its silky smooth texture and fresh taste. The consistency is quite a skill to master because it depends on the perfect *"wok hei"* (breath of wok) and the cooking time of the eggs. A lingering moment in the wok will render the eggs dry—what Cantonese chefs would describe as "old." The shrimp not only serves to complement the eggs, they enhance the overall texture of the dish. This is my take on this classic Cantonese dish. The addition of yellow chives lends a garlicky note to the overall flavor.

Serves 4–6 as part of a multicourse meal

4 oz (100 g) shelled and deveined medium-sized
  raw shrimp
6 large eggs
1 oz (30 g) yellow chives, cut into 1 in (2.5 cm)
  lengths
2½ tablespoons oil

Seasonings
½ tablespoon Chinese rice wine or sherry
¼ teaspoon sesame oil
3 dashes white pepper
½ teaspoon chicken bouillon powder
¼ teaspoon salt

1 Treat the shrimp according to "How to Make Shrimp Bouncy" on page 13. This is an optional step.
2 Crack all the eggs into a bowl and beat lightly with a pair of chopsticks.
3 Add all the ingredients for the Seasonings and the yellow chives into the eggs, beat with the chopsticks until they are blended well with the eggs, about 30 seconds.
4 Heat $1/2$ tablespoon of the oil in a wok or skillet over high heat. Stir-fry the shrimp until half-cooked or the surface turns opaque. Dish out and set aside.
5 Heat the remaining 2 tablespoons of the oil in a wok or skillet over medium heat. Pour the egg mixture gently into the wok or skillet by swirling the bowl around. Wait for 1 minute and start scrambling the eggs back and forth with the spatula. Return the shrimp to the wok or skillet and continue to scramble the eggs.
6 Turn off the heat as soon as the eggs are set and the shrimp are cooked. Dish out and serve immediately with steamed rice.

Serves 4 as part of a multicourse meal

1 block (18-oz/500 g) soft tofu, rinsed
2 tablespoons oil
2 tablespoons store-bought or homemade Chili Oil (page 27)
1 tablespoon Sichuan Peppercorn Oil (page 27)
2 cloves garlic, minced
4 oz (100 g) ground pork or beef
3 tablespoons hot bean sauce
1 teaspoon fermented black beans (douchi), rinsed and coarsely chopped
2 oz (50 g) leek or 1 stalk green onion (scallion), cut diagonally into 1 in (2.5 cm) lengths

Sauce
1 tablespoon soy sauce
1 teaspoon chili powder
½ cup (125 ml) water
Salt to taste

1 Mix all the ingredients in the Sauce in a small bowl. Set aside.
2 Cut the tofu into small bite-sized cubes, drain the water from the tofu and set aside.
3 Heat the oil, Chili Oil, and Sichuan Peppercorn Oil in a wok or skillet over high heat. Add the garlic and stir-fry to a light brown before adding the ground pork or beef, hot bean sauce, and fermented black beans. Stir the ingredients a few times until the meat is half cooked or becomes aromatic.
4 Stir in the Sauce and then add the tofu. Stir gently with the spatula to combine the ingredients well. Make sure not to break the tofu. Lower the heat and simmer for about 3–5 minutes. Add the leek or green onion and stir gently. Dish out and serve immediately with steamed rice.

> **COOK'S NOTE:** Too greasy and spicy? Tone down the oil, Chili Oil, and Sichuan Peppercorn Oil to your preference.

Mapo Tofu

I learned my Mapo Tofu recipe from a Sichuan friend, the birthplace of this remarkable dish. My friend's mother attended the Sichuan Culinary Institute at Chengdu, so the recipe is as authentic as it can be. Please be warned that this Mapo Tofu is not for the faint-hearted, it's tongue-burning fiery and downright incendiary. I just love the strong and bold flavors, however, do tone down on the chili powder and chili oil if you would like a milder taste. If you are in the mood for beef, you can use ground beef in place of ground pork.

Chinese Broccoli with Oyster Sauce

Chinese broccoli, *gailan*, is a kale-like leafy vegetable commonly found in Chinese or Asian markets. Its dark green leaves are firm to the touch, and sometimes they look as if they are coated in a thin layer of milky-colored wax. In any case, it's a much-loved Chinese vegetable. Chinese Broccoli with Oyster Sauce is the classic way of preparing this vegetable. It's so easy to prepare and yet, when cooked properly, it tastes like you spent hours in the kitchen. For this recipe, I always blanch the vegetable first before topping it with the oyster sauce. The garlic oil is optional; if used, it infuses this simple dish with an intense aroma.

Serves 4 as part of a multicourse meal

8 oz (250 g) Chinese broccoli (gailan)
Water, for boiling
¼ teaspoon oil

Garlic Oil
1 teaspoon oil
2 cloves garlic, minced

Sauce
1 tablespoon oyster sauce
1 tablespoon water
¼ teaspoon sesame oil
½ teaspoon sugar
2 dashes of white pepper

COOK'S NOTE: Older Chinese broccoli has tougher leaves and thicker stems. Blanch them for about 2 minutes. If your Chinese broccoli is younger with thinner stems, reduce the blanching time. In any case, do not overcook the Chinese broccoli. A perfectly cooked (blanched) Chinese broccoli should be green in color, not purple or overly wilted. The stems should remain somewhat crunchy.

1 Clean the Chinese broccoli thoroughly with cold water and trim off about 1 inch (2.5 cm) of the stems.
2 Prepare the Garlic Oil first by heating the oil in a wok or skillet over high heat and stir-fry the garlic until it turns light brown. Dish out the Garlic Oil and set aside.
3 Mix all the ingredients for the Sauce in a small bowl. Set aside.
4 Bring the water to a boil in a medium saucepan and add the oil. Blanch the Chinese broccoli in the boiling water. Remove the Chinese broccoli immediately with a strainer or slotted spoon as soon as they are wilted or cooked, about 1 minute. Drain the excess water. Arrange them on a serving plate.
5 Heat a saucepan over medium heat. Transfer the Sauce into the saucepan and stir to blend well. Turn off the heat as soon as the Sauce starts to bubble.
6 Pour the Sauce over the Chinese broccoli and then drizzle the Garlic Oil. Serve immediately.

Sichuan String Beans Gan Pien Si Ji Dou

I absolutely love the texture of these deep-fried string beans, my must-order vegetable dish when I dine out at Chinese restaurants. The wrinkly string bean is the result of deep-frying the beans in hot oil, and then stir-frying with dried red chilies, dried shrimp, and ground pork. The taste structure is complex—aromatic, savory, with a tint of spiciness from the dried red chilies. This dish complements other meat and seafood dishes served at a traditional multicourse Chinese meal.

Serves 2 as part of a multicourse meal

8 oz (250 g) string beans/French beans
Oil, for deep-frying
Pinch of salt
1 tablespoon oil
2 cloves garlic, minced
One ½ in (1.25 cm) piece fresh ginger,
   peeled and minced
2 oz (50 g) ground pork
1 heaping tablespoon dried shrimp,
   rinsed and coarsely chopped
6 dried red finger-length chilies, deseeded
   and cut into halves

Seasonings
¼ teaspoon chicken bouillon powder
1 teaspoon Chinese rice wine or sherry
¼ teaspoon salt
¼ teaspoon sugar

1 Clean the string beans thoroughly with cold water and trim the tips. Pat dry with paper towels and set aside.
2 Heat 2 to 3 inches (5 to 7.5 cm) of the oil in a wok or stockpot to 350°F (175°C) for deep-frying. Gently drop the string beans into the oil. As soon as the skin of the string beans becomes wrinkly, remove them with a strainer or slotted spoon, draining the excess oil by laying the string beans on a dish lined with paper towels. Season with a pinch of salt.

3 Heat 1 tablespoon of the oil in a wok or skillet over high heat. Add the garlic and ginger, and stir-fry to a light brown before adding the ground pork, dried shrimp, and dried red chilies. Stir the ingredients a few times until aromatic, and then follow with the string beans.

4 Add all the ingredients in the Seasonings and stir continuously until all the ingredients are well combined. Dish out and serve immediately with steamed rice.

Clay Pot Tofu Sha Bao Dou Fu

I love anything that is cooked in a clay pot or sand pot, and this Clay Pot Tofu is the quintessential example of this cooking method. I especially love making clay pot dishes in the winter time—the sight of a steaming hot clay pot cooking on my stove top just warms my heart as I anticipate the hot, delicious, and comforting meal.

   Chinese-style clay pots can be purchased at Chinese or Asian supermarkets or online (see Resource Guide on page 140). Don't fret if you don't have a clay pot, because a wok, stir-fry pan, or skillet will also produce satisfactory results for this Clay Pot Tofu dish.

Serves 4 as part of a multicourse meal

4 dried shiitake mushrooms

1 block (1 lb/500 g) soft or medium tofu, rinsed

Oil, for deep-frying

2 tablespoons oil

One 1 in (2.5 cm) piece fresh ginger, peeled and sliced into thin pieces

4 shelled and deveined medium-sized raw shrimp

2 oz (50 g) canned baby corns, rinsed

2 oz (50 g) Chinese (Napa) cabbage, cut into small pieces

2 oz (50 g) snow peas, tips and strings removed

Sauce

1 tablespoon soy sauce

1 tablespoon oyster sauce

1 teaspoon Chinese rice wine or sherry

½ teaspoon fish sauce

¼ teaspoon chicken bouillon powder

¼ teaspoon sesame oil

½ teaspoon sugar

3 dashes white pepper

1 tablespoon cornstarch

1 tablespoon water

1 Mix all the ingredients in the Sauce in a small bowl. Set aside.

2 Soak the dried shiitake mushrooms in warm water in a small bowl until it becomes soft. Squeeze the mushrooms dry with your hand, discard the stems, and cut the mushroom caps into halves.

3 Cut the tofu into medium-sized pieces, drain the water from the tofu, pat dry, and set aside.

4 Heat 2 to 3 inches (5 to 7.5 cm) of the oil in a wok or stockpot to 350°F (175°C) for deep-frying. Gently drop the tofu into the oil and loosen them up immediately with the spatula to prevent the tofu from clumping together.

5 Deep-fry the tofu to a light golden brown. Dish out with a strainer or slotted spoon, draining the excess oil by laying the tofu on a dish lined with paper towels. Discard or reserve the oil for use in another recipe.

6 Heat 2 tablespoons of oil in a clay pot over high heat. Add the ginger and stir-fry to a light brown before adding the shiitake mushrooms, shrimp and baby corn. Stir a few times until the shrimp is half cooked. Add the tofu, Chinese cabbage and snow peas and stir gently with the spatula to combine the ingredients well. Make sure not to break the tofu.

7 Add the Sauce, lower the heat, cover the clay pot with its lid. Simmer for about 3 minutes. Uncover the clay pot lid and stir a few times until all the ingredients are well coated with the Sauce. Dish out and serve immediately with steamed rice.

Chapter 8

Noodles and Rice

If I have any doubt at all about my Chinese heritage, I just have to remember my unreasonable dependence on rice and noodles in my daily diet. I have what I call a Chinese Mouth Syndrome (CMS)—I can go without rice and noodles for a maximum of three days before I become disoriented, and flustered!

These CMS attacks mostly occur when I travel to countries where rice and noodles are not commonly available, Europe for example. The most recent incident happened when I was at the French Riviera. After three days of indulging in some amazing French cuisine, I woke up with a craving for rice and noodles! I ended up walking around town searching madly for a Chinese or Asian restaurant. I finally found a Cambodian-Chinese cafe and ordered a helping of fried rice and chow mein. When my food came and I had the first bite, I was immediately transported to noodles and rice heaven.

Fried Rice Vermicelli with Shrimp

This dish is commonly found in Cantonese-style Chinese restaurants and noodle shops. It's one of my favorite noodle dishes especially when I have a craving for rice vermicelli. The fresh bean sprouts, onion, and green bell peppers provide great textures, while the red chili garnish adds its spiciness. Ketchup and sugar deliver a sweet-and-sour flavor that is both appetizing and mouthwatering. This recipe yields a substantial and ideal lunch dish and it's absolutely delicious.

Serves 3 as a main dish

8 oz (250 g) dried rice vermicelli
3 tablespoons oil
3 cloves garlic, finely minced
½ onion, cut into rings
4 oz (100 g) Cantonese BBQ Pork (page 81), cut into thin strips
6 shelled and deveined medium-sized raw shrimp
½ small green bell pepper, deseeded and cut into thin strips
½ small carrot, cut into thin strips
2 cups (100 g) fresh bean sprouts, ends trimmed
1 green onion (scallion), cut into 2 in (5 cm) lengths

Seasonings
1½ tablespoons oyster sauce
2 tablespoons soy sauce
2 tablespoons water
2 tablespoons ketchup
1 tablespoon sugar
¼ teaspoon sesame oil
3 dashes white pepper

Garnishing
½ teaspoon oil
1 large egg, beaten
1 red finger-length chili, deseeded and cut into thin matchstick strips

1 Soak the dried rice vermicelli in warm water to soften, about 20 minutes. Drain in a colander and set aside.

2 Mix all the ingredients for the Seasonings in a small bowl. Set aside.

3 To prepare the Garnishing, heat the wok or skillet over medium heat and add the oil. Fry the egg into a thin omelet. Remove from the heat and let it cool, roll it up and slice thinly.

4 Heat the oil in a wok or skillet over high heat. Add the garlic, onion, and stir-fry until aromatic, then follow with the Cantonese BBQ Pork, shrimp, green bell pepper, and carrot. Continue to stir-fry until the shrimp are half cooked.

5 Add the rice vermicelli and the Seasonings, toss and swirl the rice vermicelli with the spatula until the Seasonings are absorbed and the vermicelli are no longer wet, about 2–3 minutes. Add the bean sprouts and green onion, and continue stir-frying until the bean sprouts are cooked and well combined with the vermicelli, about 1 minute. Remove from the heat and transfer the rice vermicelli to a serving platter.

6 Garnish the rice vermicelli with the omelet strips and red chili strips. Serve immediately.

Classic Shrimp Fried Rice

Fried rice is potentially one of the most-ordered Chinese dishes in the world and the reasons are quite obvious: it's convenient, affordable, and packed with nutrition and flavors. There are numerous variations of fried rice recipes, but I am partial to shrimp fried rice. Everything seems to taste better with fresh, succulent, and luscious shrimp; Classic Shrimp Fried Rice is no exception. When dining out at Chinese restaurants, don't be shy about asking for more steamed white rice to go with your order. I always bring home the extra rice from restaurants and fry up a batch of Classic Shrimp Fried Rice the next day. For best results, the rice should be chilled in a refrigerator overnight (hence "overnight rice") before the cooking process.

Serves 2 as a main dish or 4 as part of a
   multicourse meal

3 cups (500 g) overnight steamed white
   rice
2½ tablespoons oil
3 large eggs, beaten and seasoned with a
   pinch of salt
2 cloves garlic, minced
One ½ in (1.25 cm) piece fresh ginger,
   peeled and minced
4 oz (100 g) shelled and deveined
   medium-sized raw shrimp
1 cup (160 g) store-bought frozen peas
   and carrots
Salt, to taste

Seasonings
1½ tablespoons soy sauce
½ tablespoon fish sauce
¼ teaspoon sesame oil
3 dashes white pepper

1 Gently break up the lumpy overnight rice with the back of a spoon or fork. Mix all the ingredients for the Seasonings in a small bowl. Set aside.

2 Heat ¹/₂ tablespoon of the oil in a wok or skillet over high heat. Gently pour in the beaten eggs and fry until it just starts to set, about 1 minute. Flip the egg over and continue to fry until it's set. Use the spatula to break the eggs into small pieces. Dish out and set aside.

3 Reheat the wok or skillet over high heat and add the remaining 2 tablespoons of oil. Add the minced garlic and ginger, stir-fry until they become light brown in color or aromatic.

4 Add the shrimp and stir-fry until they are half-cooked or the surface turns opaque, and then add the frozen peas and carrots. Stir quickly to combine the ingredients, about 10 seconds. Spoon the rice into the wok or skillet and combine everything evenly with a spatula.

5 Stir in the Seasonings, blending it well with the rice. Return the cooked eggs to the wok or skillet, stir to combine with the rice and cook the rice. Keep stirring the fried rice until slightly toasted, about 3 minutes. Add salt to taste, dish out and serve immediately.

Yangzhou Fried Rice

My earliest memories of Yangzhou Fried Rice came from the many Chinese banquets I attended while I was in Malaysia. Yangzhou Fried Rice would always be served towards the end of the multicourse banquet, usually as the 7th course, right before the dessert. By the time it was served, most guests would be quite stuffed and usually, they would not even touch it. I loved Yangzhou Fried Rice, especially the diced ham—they were like little treasures buried in the rice. I would be picking them out and savoring them, without having to fight the other guests for a healthy share of this rice dish. If you don't like ham, you can make Yangzhou Fried Rice with diced Cantonese BBQ Pork (page 81), a common variation of this classic Chinese recipe.

Serves 2 as a main dish or 4 as part of a multicourse meal

3 cups (500 g) overnight steamed white rice
2½ tablespoons oil
3 large eggs, beaten and seasoned with a pinch of salt
3 cloves garlic, minced
5 oz (150 g) ham, diced
½ cup (80 g) store-bought frozen peas and carrots
Salt, to taste

Seasonings
½ tablespoon soy sauce
1½ tablespoons fish sauce
¼ teaspoon sesame oil
3 dashes white pepper

1 Gently break up the lumpy overnight rice with the back of a spoon or fork.

2 Mix all the ingredients for the Seasonings in a small bowl. Set aside.

3 Heat $1/2$ tablespoon of the oil in a wok or skillet over high heat. Gently pour in the beaten eggs and fry until it just starts to set, about 1 minute. Flip the egg over and continue to fry until it's set. Use the spatula to break the eggs into small pieces. Dish out and set aside.

4 Reheat the wok or skillet over high heat and add the remaining 2 tablespoons of the oil. Add the minced garlic, stir-fry until they become light brown in color or aromatic.

5 Add the ham and stir-fry until the surface is slightly charred, and then add the frozen peas and carrots. Stir quickly to combine the ingredients, about 10 seconds. Spoon the rice into the wok or skillet and combine everything evenly with the spatula.

6 Stir in the Seasonings, blending it well with the rice. Return the cooked eggs to the wok or skillet, stir to combine with the rice. Keep stirring the fried rice until slightly toasted, about 3 minutes. Add salt to taste, dish out and serve immediately.

> **COOK'S NOTE:** There are many variations of Yangzhou Fried Rice. Cantonese cooks use Cantonese BBQ Pork in place of ham. You can also use frozen peas solely for this dish instead of frozen peas and carrots.

Serves 3 as a main dish

1½ lbs (750 g) fresh flat rice noodles
2½ tablespoons oil
1 tablespoon soy sauce
2 cloves garlic, minced
6 shelled and deveined medium-sized raw
   shrimp
2 oz (50 g) fish fillet, 1 in (2.5 cm) thick, cut
   into bite-sized pieces
2 oz (50 g) bay scallops
2 oz (50 g) cleaned squid, cut into rings
2 oz (50 g) baby bok choy, cut lengthwise
   into halves
2 oz (50 g) canned straw mushrooms, rinsed
½ small carrot, sliced into pieces
Handful yellow chives, cut into 2 in (5 cm)
   lengths
Pickled Green Chilies (page 28), to serve

Sauce
1 cup (250 ml) Homemade Chicken Stock
   (page 31) or store-bought chicken broth
1 cup (250 ml) water
3 dashes white pepper
½ teaspoon sesame oil
½ teaspoon sugar
½ tablespoon fish sauce
2 tablespoons cornstarch
1 teaspoon Chinese rice wine or sherry
¾ teaspoon salt or to taste

Seafood Chow Fun Noodles

There are two ways of preparing noodles the Cantonese way: dry stir-fry and wet stir-fry. Dry stir-fry means that the noodles are served without a sauce, like Beef Chow Fun Noodles (page 123). Wet stir-fry means that the noodles are doused in a sauce or gravy.

This Seafood Chow Fun Noodles is a great illustration of Cantonese wet stir-fry. The rice noodles are pan-fried first and a white and slightly thick sauce laced with various seafoods is then poured on top of the bed of noodles.

I love eating this dish with Pickled Green Chilies (page 28), which adds a spicy and vinegary zing to the overall taste.

1 Loosen the flat rice noodles completely so they don't clump together. Heat 1 tablespoon of the oil in a wok or skillet over high heat. Add the noodle and soy sauce and stir-fry until slightly charred. Transfer the noodles to a deep serving plate or bowl.
2 Mix all the ingredients for the Sauce in a small bowl. Set aside.
3 Heat the remaining oil in a wok or skillet over high heat. Add in the minced garlic and stir-fry to a light brown and then pour in the Sauce.
4 Add the shrimp, fish, bay scallops, squid, baby bok choy, straw mushrooms, carrot, and yellow chives and bring the Sauce to a boil. Pour the Sauce on top of the flat rice noodles. Serve hot with Pickled Green Chilies.

4–6 oz (100–175 g) beef tenderloin, cut into bite-sized pieces
1 lb (500 g) fresh flat rice noodles
1½–2 tablespoons oil
2 cloves garlic, minced
1 cup (100 g) fresh bean sprouts, ends trimmed
1 oz (50 g) green onion (scallion) or yellow chives, cut into 2 in (5 cm) lengths

Marinade
1 teaspoon soy sauce
¼ teaspoon dark soy sauce
½ teaspoon Chinese rice wine or sherry
1 heaping teaspoon cornstarch

Seasonings
2 tablespoons soy sauce
¼ teaspoon dark soy sauce
1 tablespoon oyster sauce
½ teaspoon fish sauce
¼ teaspoon sugar

1 Treat the beef according to "How to Tenderize Meat" on page 12. This is an optional step.
2 Marinate the beef with the Marinade for 15 minutes.
3 Loosen the flat rice noodles completely so they don't clump together.
4 Mix all the ingredients for the Seasonings in a small bowl. Set aside.
5 Heat the oil in a wok or skillet over high heat. Add the garlic and stir-fry until a light brown. Add the beef and stir-fry until they are half-cooked, and then follow with the bean sprouts, flat rice noodles, and the Seasonings.
6 Toss and swirl the flat rice noodles with the spatula until the Seasonings are well combined with the noodles. Continue stir-frying until the noodles are slightly charred, about 1–2 minutes. Add the green onion or yellow chives and stir-fry for another 10 seconds.
7 Remove from the heat and transfer the Beef Chow Fun Noodles to a serving platter. Serve immediately.

Beef Chow Fun Noodles

Beef Chow Fun Noodles is made with flat rice noodles. I always get the cut version because of the convenience; all I do is loosen up the noodles by hand so they don't clump together while cooking. My favorite Beef Chow Fun Noodles can be found in Salt Lake City, at Little World Chinese Restaurant, a tiny hole-in-the-wall Chinese eatery. It was spectacular—infused with generous *wok hei* (breath of wok), a sublime balance of taste and aroma. My husband and I would still muse over that glorious Beef Chow Fun and joked about the waitress who always mispronounced its Cantonese name. One of these days, we will have to head back to Salt Lake City for a fix.

COOK'S NOTE: Some fresh flat rice noodles are oilier than others, so the amount of the oil used for this recipe is up to your liking. Beef Chow Fun Noodles should be slightly oily nonetheless.

Shanghai Fried Noodles

In the local neighborhoods or markets of Shanghai, you will run into fried noodles vendors frying up a pile of Shanghai noodles in a round flat griddle, using long wooden chopsticks to constantly toss and stir the glistening noodles.

The cooking process is as fascinating to me as the taste of the noodles. Shanghai noodles are usually thicker and chewier than other noodles providing a great texture when stir-fried with the simple ingredients of pork and vegetables. While most Chinese or Cantonese-style noodles are often fried with minced garlic, authentic Shanghai fried noodles go without it. My Shanghainese friend who runs a restaurant told me that Shanghainese are not big fans of garlic but they like their food greasy, sweet and salty with bold flavors. For my recipe, I cut down on the grease to ensure a healthier dish. You can get the noodles from Chinese food stores where they are labeled as Shanghai noodles. If you can't find Shanghai noodles, you can use any thick noodles or even udon as a substitute.

Serves 2 as a main dish

4 oz (100 g) pork, cut into thin strips
1 teaspoon Chinese rice wine or sherry
½ teaspoon soy sauce
½ teaspoon cornstarch
Water, for boiling
1 lb (500 g) fresh Shanghai noodles or thick noodles
2 tablespoons oil
4 oz (100 g) fresh spinach, stemmed and washed
1 green onion (scallion), trimmed and cut into small rounds

Seasonings
2 tablespoons soy sauce
1 tablespoon dark soy sauce
1 tablespoon sugar
3 dashes white pepper
¼ teaspoon salt or to taste

1 Marinate the pork with the rice wine or sherry, soy sauce, and cornstarch for 10 minutes.

2 Mix all the ingredients for the Seasonings in a small bowl and set aside.

3 Bring the water to a boil in a pot. Boil the noodles for 5 minutes, drain and run cold water over the noodles for 30 seconds. Set aside.

4 Heat ½ tablespoon of the oil in a wok or skillet over high heat. Add the pork and then stir-fry for 1 minute. Dish out and set aside.

5 After cleaning the wok or skillet, use it to heat the remaining oil over high heat. Add the noodles and the Seasonings and stir to blend well.

6 Return the pork to the wok or skillet. Add the spinach and then stir-fry until the spinach combines well with the noodles and becomes wilted, about 1 minute. Add the green onion, stir and remove from the heat. Serve immediately.

Homestyle Chow Mein Noodles

Chow Mein is one of the earliest Chinese dishes introduced to America and its popularity hasn't waned. One of the most popular take-out items at Chinese restaurants, Chow Mein is synonymous with great food, convenience, and affordability. The mental picture of eating Chow Mein packed in a Chinese take-out box, with a pair of disposable wooden chopsticks while watching TV is as American as having wings during the Super Bowl. Chow Mein is an American food icon despite its Chinese origin. This Homestyle Chow Mein Noodles recipe is a healthy take on your favorite version—less greasy, more ingredients, and no MSG.

Serves 2 as a main dish or 4 as part of a
  multicourse meal

8 oz (250 g) steamed chow mein noodles
2 oz (50 g) pork, cut into thin slices
⅓ teaspoon soy sauce
¼ teaspoon cornstarch
2 tablespoons oil
3 cloves garlic, minced
6 shelled and deveined medium-sized raw
  shrimp
⅓ cup (50 g) shredded cabbage
⅓ cup (50 g) shredded carrot
2 cups (100 g) fresh bean sprouts, ends
  trimmed
2 tablespoons water
2 green onions (scallions), cut into 2 in
  (5 cm) length
Salt, to taste

Seasonings
1 tablespoon soy sauce
1 tablespoon oyster sauce
½ teaspoon sugar
½ teaspoon dark soy sauce
2 tablespoons water

1 Rinse the steamed noodles with cold running water a few times until the water turns clear and the noodles become soft. Drain the excess water with a colander and set aside. (Do not clean them for too long or the noodles will become soggy.)

2 Mix all the ingredients for the Seasonings in a small bowl. Set aside.

3 Marinate the pork with the soy sauce and cornstarch in a bowl, for 10 minutes.

4 Heat the oil in a wok or skillet over high heat. When the oil starts to smoke, add in the minced garlic and stir-fry until the garlic is light brown or aromatic. Add the pork and shrimp and stir-fry until they are half-cooked or the surface turns opaque.

5 Stir in the shredded cabbage, carrot, and bean sprouts into the wok, stirring well with the other ingredients in the wok or skillet.

6 Add the noodles, the Seasonings, and the water. Stir continuously until the noodles are well combined with the Seasonings and cook thoroughly.

7 Add the chopped green onion and salt to taste. Toss well with the noodles, dish out and serve immediately.

Crispy Pan-fried Noodles

This is a notable Cantonese noodle dish where the noodles are fried to a crispy golden brown before a savory sauce is poured over them. The end result is a plate of crispy noodles coated with a light sauce and topped with tasty ingredients such as bok choy, meat, and shrimp. Every bite has an inviting crunch, and then the noodles slowly soften in your mouth. I simply love the texture of this noodle dish. In Chinese restaurants, the noodles are basically deep-fried, but at home, you can just shallow fry them with a pan. Make sure to drain the excess oil off the noodles with paper towels so that the bottom part of the noodles isn't drenched in oil.

Serves 2 as a main dish

Water, for boiling
8 oz (250 g) steamed chow mein
2 oz (50 g) beef, cut into pieces
2 oz (50 g) chicken meat, cut into pieces
4 tablespoons oil
2 cloves garlic, minced
6 shelled and deveined medium-sized raw
   shrimp
2 oz (50) baby bok choy
½ small carrot, sliced into pieces
Handful of yellow chives, cut into 2 in
   (5 cm) lengths
Pickled Green Chilies (page 28), to serve

Marinade
1 teaspoon soy sauce
½ teaspoon rice wine or sherry
1 teaspoon starch

Sauce
1 cup (250 ml) Homemade Chicken Stock
   (page 31) or store-bought chicken broth
1 cup (250 ml) water
½ teaspoon sesame oil
½ teaspoon sugar
½ tablespoon fish sauce
3 dashes white pepper
1½ tablespoons cornstarch
¼ teaspoon salt or to taste

1 Bring the water to a boil and blanch the steamed chow mein for 10 seconds or per the packaging instruction. Remove the steamed chow mein, drain and air dry for 15 minutes.

2 Marinate the beef and chicken with all the ingredients in the Marinade, for 15 minutes.

3 Mix all the ingredients for the Sauce in a small bowl. Set aside.

4 Heat 2 tablespoons of the oil in a wok or skillet over high heat. Lay the chow mein on an even layer on the wok or skillet. Lower the heat to medium and shallow-fry until crispy, about 2–3 minutes. Flip the chow mein over, add another 1 tablespoon of the oil, and fry until crispy, for another 2–3 minutes. Transfer the chow mein to a dish lined with paper towels to drain the excess oil. Transfer the drained chow mein to a deep serving plate.

5 Heat the remaining oil in a wok or skillet over high heat. Add in the minced garlic and stir-fry to a light brown and then pour in the Sauce.

6 Add the shrimp, beef, chicken, baby bok choy, carrot, and yellow chives and bring the Sauce to a boil. Pour the Sauce on top of the chow mein. Serve hot with Pickled Green Chilies.

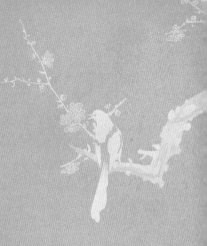

Chapter 9

Desserts and Drinks

There is an old stereotype that Chinese desserts are dull and uninteresting, but I disagree. Even though dessert is not really a vital part of Chinese cuisine, it's not without its varieties. In fact, Chinese desserts can include sweet stuffed pancakes, soothing drinks, cooling shaved ice, pastry and tarts, rice or sticky-rice based decadent desserts, which are, nonetheless, quite different from the western definition of desserts.

Here are some of my favorite Chinese desserts and drinks designed to complete your meal on a sweet note.

Sweet Peanut Nuggets

This recipe is adapted from a classic Chinese recipe called "*tang bu sh-uai*." This dessert is a decadent delight. Legend has it that in ancient China, the family of a single woman would serve this dessert to the potential groom to signify the beginning of a sweet and happy marriage. I am not sure about the truth of this tale, but I am sure you will love this addictive and delicious recipe.

Makes 24 nuggets

8 oz (250 g) glutinous (sticky) rice flour
¾ cup (185 ml) water
Water, for boiling
3 tablespoons roasted peanuts, coarsely chopped, to garnish

Coating
3 oz (75 g) ground peanut
3 oz (75 g) fine sugar
2 tablespoons white sesame seeds, lightly toasted

1 Add the glutinous rice flour into a big bowl and pour the water in slowly, kneading it while adding the water until it becomes a dough. The dough is ready when it's no longer sticky and the surface becomes smooth, about 10 minutes. Cover the dough with a damp cloth and let it rest for 30 minutes.
2 Divide the dough into two equal portions and roll the portions into two cylinders. Cut each cylinder into 12 equal pieces.
3 Gently roll each piece of the dough into a ball shape using both palms.
4 Mix all the ingredients for the Coating in a bowl until thoroughly blended. Set aside.
5 Bring the water to a boil in a pot. Gently transfer the glutinous rice balls into the boiling water and boil until they float to the top, about 2 minutes.
6 Remove the rice balls with a strainer or slotted spoon, shake off the excess water and then coat them generously with the Coating. Garnish the nuggets with the chopped roasted peanuts and serve immediately.

> **COOK'S NOTE:** Depending on the glutinous rice flour you use, you might need more or less water. If the dough is too watery, add more glutinous rice flour. If the dough is too dry, add more water.

Fresh Mango Pudding Mang Guo Bu Ding

Mango pudding is a common dessert served after Chinese banquet dinners or at dim sum meals. Though the ingredients might not be Chinese, it is popular with Chinese food lovers. The bright flavor of ripe mangos is given a creamy touch by the evaporated milk. Unflavored gelatin—which you can find at any supermarket—acts as the binding agent to set the pudding. I always serve my mango pudding with some extra evaporated milk, along with a garnish, such as blackberries, diced mangos, or other fruit.

Makes 6

1 lb (500 g) peeled and deseeded ripe mango, cut
   into small pieces
½ cup (125 ml) evaporated milk plus 6 tablespoons
   (for topping)
1 cup (250 ml) hot water
½ cup (100 g) sugar
1½ tablespoons unflavored gelatin
3 ice cubes
Blackberries, diced kiwi or mango, to garnish

1 Blend the mango in an electronic blender until it becomes a smooth puree. The mango yields about 1³/4 cups (425 ml) mango puree.
2 Add the evaporated milk into the mango puree and stir to mix well.
3 Combine the hot water, sugar, and gelatin in another container. Stir continuously to blend well. Make sure the gelatin dissolves completely.
4 Add the ice cubes to the mango puree. Pour the sugar mixture into the puree and keep stirring until the ice cubes melt away. Filter the mango puree with a fine-mesh strainer.
5 Transfer the mango puree into six 6-ounce (177 ml)-sized custard cups. Chill in the refrigerator for at least 3 hours or until the mango puddings are set.
6 Top each mango pudding with 1 tablespoon of evaporated milk before serving. Garnish with diced mango or fruit as you desire. Serve immediately.

> **COOK'S NOTE:** Depending on the sweetness of the mangos you use, you might want to adjust the quantity of the sugar used.

Shaved Ice with Fresh Fruits

In recent years, shaved ice has certainly gained popularity in the United States, with many Chinese dessert shops sprouting up all over Chinatown or Asian suburbs. You don't have to live in one of those areas to enjoy this refreshing and soothing dessert. I really love this simple recipe: finely shaved and snowy ice, flavored with syrup and topped with an assortment of fruits. It is a cooling dessert and an excellent thirst quencher for warm summer days.

Serves 4

4 cups (500 g) ice cubes or crushed ice
4 tablespoons condensed milk or
   evaporated milk

Syrup (yields about 8 tablespoons)
½ cup (100 g) dark brown sugar
⅓ cup (80 ml) water

Toppings
1 cup (175 g) diced mango
1 cup (175 g) diced kiwi
4 strawberries, sliced into pieces

1 Heat up a saucepan over medium heat and bring the ingredients in the Syrup to a boil, stirring continuously. Turn off the heat as soon as the dark brown sugar dissolves. Set aside and let cool.
2 Shave the ice cubes or crushed ice in a blender.
3 Divide the shaved ice equally into 4 ice cream cups.
4 Add 1 tablespoon condensed milk and 2 tablespoons syrup into each shaved ice.
5 Top each shaved ice with ¼ portion of diced mango, ¼ portion kiwi, and ¼ portion of strawberry. Serve immediately.

Sweet Boba Milk Tea Bo Ba Nai Cha

Tea has always been the beverage of choice for the Chinese people and green tea is particularly popular because of its many health and medical benefits. Every time I visit China I always bring back bottles of tea leaves with me. I prefer Chinese green tea leaves such as *longjing*, or Dragon Well, for this drink. The distinct fragrance and lingering aroma of the tea, combined with evaporated milk, honey, and chewy tapioca pearls is delightful and invigorating, especially after a heavy meal. You can substitute *longjing* with any Chinese green tea of your choice, but I would stay away from powdered green tea because it's not the best choice for this soothing drink.

Makes 4 glasses

½ cup (75 g) tapioca pearls or boba
3 cups (750 ml) water
3 tablespoons green tea leaves
8 tablespoons evaporated milk
8 tablespoons honey
Ice cubes or crushed ice

1 Prepare the tapioca pearls according to the packaging instructions. Rinse and drain the boiled tapioca pearls in cold water. Set aside.
2 Bring the water to a boil and remove from the heat, then add the green tea leaves. Set aside for 20–30 minutes to allow the tea to release its fragrance and aroma into the water.
3 Strain the tea into a pitcher and discard the tea leaves. It should yield about 2 cups (500 ml) of green tea.
4 Add the evaporated milk, honey, and tapioca pearls and mix well with the tea. Pour the Sweet Boba Milk Tea into four glasses. Add some ice cubes and serve cold.

Flaky Sweet Egg Tarts Dan Ta

This Flaky Sweet Egg Tarts recipe took me many trials and errors to adapt and perfect. When making egg tarts, there is the common problem of the custard sinking after the egg tarts are removed from the oven. I consulted a number of people to ensure my recipe works precisely and that the egg custard filling doesn't deflate. Here is the simple key to "no sink" egg tarts: do not whisk the egg custard mixture, because whisking incorporates too much air to the filling.

I would like to dedicate this recipe to Jaden Hair of *The Steamy Kitchen Cookbook*, who loves these sweet treats. Special thanks to pastry chef Betty Trinidad for the valuable "no sink custard" tips, Siew Loon for providing me with the original recipe, and the many testers (Debbie, Ju, Pick Yin) who helped refine this recipe.

Makes 24 tarts

Butter, for greasing

Filling
6 large eggs
2 cups (500 ml) milk
6 oz (175 g) sugar
½ teaspoon vanilla extract

Pastry
8 oz (250 g) butter
1 large egg, lightly beaten
12 oz (350 g) all-purpose flour, sifted
2 oz (50 g) confectioners' sugar

1 To make the Filling, beat the eggs very gently with a fork in a bowl. Do not whisk. Mix the rest of the ingredients in a separate bowl until the sugar is completely dissolved. Stir in the beaten eggs to mix well. Strain the Filling using a fine mesh strainer slowly. Repeat 2 to 3 times. Make sure the surface of the Filling has no air bubbles. Chill the Filling in the refrigerator for 30 minutes.
2 Mix all the Pastry ingredients together and knead it into dough using your hands, about 10–15 minutes. The dough is ready when it no longer sticks to your fingers.
3 Grease the tart molds (3 inches/7.5 cm in diameter) with some butter.

4 Divide the dough into 24 dough balls and press them into the molds. The pastry should be thin because the dough puffs up slightly after baking.
5 Preheat the oven to 325°F (160°C). Pre-bake the pastry first, about 10–15 minutes.
6 Remove the tart molds from the oven and gently pour the Filling into each tart mold, about 90% full. Make sure there are no air bubbles forming on the surface of the Filling.
7 Bake the egg tarts at 325°F (160°C) for about 20–30 minutes, or until the Filling is set. Check at the 20–minute mark for doneness.
8 Remove the egg tarts from the oven, let cool for 5–10 minutes. Loosen the egg tarts from the molds and serve warm.

COOK'S NOTES: For best results, follow the American measurement here because this recipe needs to be very precise. The metrics conversion has been rounded up.

You can halve all the ingredients and make 12 tarts.

In warm weather, chill the dough (after you have pressed them into the tart molds) for 10 minutes before baking.

Red Bean Pancakes

When I was a child, my cousin would come stay with us during school holidays. One year, he became an apprentice at a Chinese restaurant and every night after work, he would return with his creations. My favorite was Red Bean Pancakes—a crepe like pancake stuffed with sweet red bean paste, deep-fried to golden brown, and speckled with sesame seeds.

In the past, I had to make the red bean paste from scratch, which takes hours! Nowadays, I am just as happy with the store-bought, canned, sweetened red bean paste, which is far more convenient and delivers terrific results.

Makes 3 pieces

1 cup (130 g) all-purpose flour, sifted
1 cup (250 ml) water
1 large egg
1½ teaspoons oil, for pan-frying
6 tablespoons canned sweeten (mashed) red bean paste
3 teaspoons white sesame seeds
Oil, for deep-frying

1 Mix the all-purpose flour, water, and egg to yield 1^1/$_2$ cups (375 ml) batter. Strain the batter and divide the batter into 3 equal portions.
2 Heat ^{1}/$_2$ teaspoon of the oil in an 8-inch (20 cm) flat, non-stick frying pan over low heat. Swirl the oil around so the bottom of the pan is well coated with the oil.
3 Pour one portion of the batter into the frying pan. Tilt and swirl it to let the batter coat evenly to form a thin 8-inch (20 cm) pancake. Cook for about 2 minutes, or until the pancake is set. Do not turn the pancake over. Loosen the edges using a spatula; lift the pancake to a flat surface.

4 Repeat step 2–3 for the other two pancakes.
5 Spread 2 tablespoons of the canned red bean paste on the pancake, starting at the lower center, leaving about 1 inch (2.5 cm) on both left and right sides and the bottom side. Fold the bottom side over the red bean paste and seal the sides and edges with the leftover batter, forming a 5 x 4-inch (12.75 x 10 cm) rectangle. Repeat the same for the other two pancakes.
6 Sprinkle 1 teaspoon of the white sesame seeds on the surface of the pancakes. Then seal the pancake with the leftover batter.
7 Heat 2 to 3 inches (5 to 7.5 cm) of the oil in a wok or stockpot to 350°F (175°C). Gently drop the pancake into the oil, one at a time.
8 Deep-fry until the pancake turns light golden brown. Dish out with a strainer or slotted spoon, draining the excess oil by laying the pancakes on a wire rack or a dish lined with paper towels. Cut each pancake into pieces and serve immediately.

> **COOK'S NOTE:** Make sure the pancake is tightly sealed. Loosely sealed pancakes will break open during deep-frying.

Acknowledgments

If you had asked me five years ago if I had ever thought about writing a cookbook, the answer would be an absolute NO. But great things happened after July 2006, after I started my food blog, Rasa Malaysia (http://rasamalaysia.com). The site soon bloomed into one of the most popular Asian food blogs on the web, with hundreds of thousands of readers and growing traffic every month.

In July 2009, three years after the launch of Rasa Malaysia, I got an email from my editor Bud Sperry of Tuttle Publishing, who asked me if I would be interested in doing a Chinese cookbook. I jumped at the opportunity without any hesitation, and the rest, as you would say, is history.

I have to say that I have been extremely lucky regarding this project. I wasn't subjected to the painful process of writing a proposal, finding a literary agent, and shopping for a deal. It just sort of landed on my lap. However, this cookbook wouldn't have been possible if not for the support and love I have received from so many people. This includes my dear husband, G, who always believes in me and lets me pursue my every dream, all my family members back in Malaysia, especially my two sisters, my fans and readers from all over the world, and of course, my adorable baby G, who lightens up my day and is a constant reminder that I am truly blessed.

To my two good friends in Southern California: Shirley Lim, who gave me endless advice and tips, and to Farina Carr, who is always so much fun to be with. I won't forget all my good friends back home in Malaysia, Bee Ean, Wai Wan, and Joanne, who give me their support, albeit remotely. To Siew Loon, for buying me props whenever she travels, and most importantly, for helping me earnestly without ever asking for anything in return. And to my dear friend Jim Doane, who always encourages me in everything I do, and to Albert Biscarra, for your editing help during the early phase of this project. To Chef Alex Ong of Betelnut Restaurant in San Francisco, who always tries to help me with my culinary career.

Special thanks go to Jaden Hair of *The Steamy Kitchen Cookbook* for writing the Foreword of this cookbook and her continued support and friendship since we first met in 2007. To Robert and Esther Danhi, for loaning me your pre-

cious props and sharing your "insider" recipes. To Alice and Jared Zhao, of Zhao Photography, for taking the gorgeous ingredients shots. Also to Diane Cu and Todd Porter, whose portrait photography makes me look like a domestic goddess who can sell cookbooks!

To Robyn Eckhardt of Eating Asia (http://eatingasia.typepad.com) who is always an email away whenever I need an advice or just to vent. To acclaimed Chinese cookbook author Grace Young, who is so warm, friendly, and whose cookbooks inspired me to work on my own. To acclaimed authors cum food writers Andrea Nguyen, who encouraged me to write and shared food writing resources with me; and to Harris Salat, who gave me sound advice when I first started working on the book.

To Eleanor Hoh, who wrote the section about "Seasoning a Cast Iron Wok" on page 19. To Shao Zhi Zhong (http://www.friedwontons4u.com), Kamran Siddiqi (http://www.sophisticatedgourmet.com), and Jason Tong (http://www.jasontongphotography.com) for helping me with the mundane and boring blog-related chores when I was buried in this project. To Rachael Hutchings of Fujimama (http://www.lafujimama.com) who went props shopping with me; to Matt Wright of Wright Food (http://mattikaarts.com/blog/) who gave me food photography advice. To my Twitter friends Brian Lew and David Nguyen, for always being so kind and sweet. To Carolyn Shek, for tasting my food and taking Chinatown photos for me. And to all my fellow food bloggers for your encouraging words on my website, Facebook, Twitter, and email.

I would like to thank all my recipe testers—especially Debbie Wong and Irene Chan, who tested and retested many of my recipes—I can't thank you all enough for your warm participation, honest feedback, and candid input.

Alexandra Taylor	Ann Lee Ling	Chee Ann Williams
Allison Day	Brian Lew	Cheryl Ng Collett
Amanda Zimmer	Camila Santos	Dana Stradley
Ananthi Parkin	Guimarães	Debb Odell
Angie Ma	Carole Kweon	Dennis Glorioso
Anh Sawh	Chang Pick Yin	Eleanor Hoh

Ellie Hoeve	Kamran Siddiqi	Rachael Hutchings
Erika Pineda	Karina A Santos	Rachel Nishimura
Esther Danhi	Katherine Dierking	Ravien Sewtahal
Finla Noronha	Khoo Ling Tze	Robin Kok
François Lacoste	Kim Davidson	Rose Muralla
Gary Cote	Kok Robin	Sarah Mak
Goh Yih Lin	Lawrence Parks	Shao Zhi Zhong
Guillermo Fernandez Castellanos	Leslie Gross Wyrtzen	Sharon Natasha Pious
Heng Ju-ee	Lim Swee San	Sherene Khaw
Ho Siew Loon	Lucy Tran	Siew Hoon Yeoh
Hui Leng Tay	Marion Dumas	Sophanny Sok
Jason Tong	Marja Allen	Su Khoon Kwan
Jeffrey Siaw	Maud Christensen	Su Low
Jennifer Mar	Michelle Huynh	Sumeet Nair
Jenny Kayano	Mung Sar Tan	Trissa Lopez
Jit Fong Chin	Nor Aini Adnan	Vonny Groose
Joanna Meyer	Pablo Jimenez	Wendy Leung
Joanna Repeć	Paula Jones	Mountainbear
Josephine Lim	Penny Cai	Zoe Chan
Julie Wan	Peter Catchpole	
Justin Timbers	Quyen Gin	

Last but not least, I must thank the team at Tuttle and Periplus for working with me on this project: Eric Oey, Bud Sperry, June Chong, Irene Ho, Christopher Johns, Gail Tok, and Rowan Muelling-Auer.

If I have left out any of you in this chapter, I am sincerely sorry for my omission.

Thank you all so much, or in Mandarin, *xie xie*!

Resource Guide

Here are my favorite collections of Chinese cookbooks. I truly respect the work of Grace Young and Eileen Yin-Fei Lo and their books are my go-to resources whenever I have doubts or need information about a certain Chinese ingredient, cooking method, or recipe. Grace Young's in-depth research and works on wok and stir-frying are brilliant and inspiring, while Eileen's latest cookbook *Mastering the Art of Chinese Cooking* is the ultimate guide to learning Chinese cuisine. Martin Yan's recipes are always fun and creative while Fuschia Dunlop's dedication to Sichuan and Hunan cuisines—two of my favorite Chinese regional cuisines—are simply fascinating. I am a huge fan of Jeffrey Alford and Naomi Duguid and their cookbooks are such treasures, both visually stunning and deeply engaging. Last but not least, Cecilia Chiang is the legendary figure in Chinese cooking, who has been credited with introducing authentic Chinese cuisines to the United States through her restaurant and literary works.

Chinese Cookbooks

The Breath of a Wok by Grace Young

Stir-frying to the Sky's Edge by Grace Young

Beyond the Great Wall: Recipes and Travels in the Other China by Jeffrey Alford and Naomi Duguid

The Seventh Daughter: My Culinary Journey from Beijing to San Francisco by Cecilia Chiang

Mastering the Art of Chinese Cooking by Eileen Yin-Fei Lo

Martin Yan's China by Martin Yan

Land of Plenty: A Treasury of Authentic Sichuan Cooking by Fuschia Dunlop

Revolutionary Chinese Cookbook: Recipes from Hunan Province by Fuschia Dunlop

Chinese Utensils and Tools

The Wok Shop
www.wokshop.com/store

Wok Star
wokstar.us

Asian Markets Database

New Asian Cuisine
www.newasiancuisine.com

Online Retailers for Chinese Ingredients

Asian Supermarket 365
www.asiansupermarket365.com

Ethnic Food Co.
store.ethnicfoodsco.com

Asian Wok
www.asianwok.com

Amazon
www.amazon.com

Wing Yip Online Store (UK)
www.wingyipstore.co.uk

About Food Styling and Photography

All the photos in this cookbook, with the exception of the ingredients shots, are single-handedly styled and photographed by yours truly.

To prepare myself for cookbook-worthy food photography, I invested in a professional and full frame DSLR camera—the wildly popular Canon 5D Mark II as soon as I started working on the book. I also purchased a couple of great lenses for food photography and a tripod for the camera. I don't have a professional studio at home; my workspace is my dining table beside the side windows, which are taped with a layer of vellum paper to diffuse the natural light—a trick I've learned from Matt Wright of Wright Food.

Even with the right gear and equipment, I have to acknowledge that food styling and photography for this cookbook had proven to be far more challenging than I had originally anticipated. While I shoot pretty decent photos on my food blog at Rasa Malaysia (rasamalaysia.com), food styling and photography for print and cookbook demand a completely different skill set, one that I unfortunately lack: professional composition of shots, lighting, set up, propping, styling, and a pair of keen and artistic eyes. Each photo has to be unique and convey a certain "mood." They also have to be refined, perfected, and most importantly, the finished dishes have to look inviting and awaken the reader's appetite.

My biggest struggle was food styling, mostly because I don't have a storeroom full of props to play or get creative with. Because of that, I developed a serious case of props envy whenever I flipped through my favorite cookbooks, food magazines, or whenever I visited gorgeous food blogs or websites.

I had spent hundreds of dollars buying props for my cookbook, but they just weren't enough. Luckily, my friend Chef Robert Danhi came to my rescue by loaning his precious props to me. I would like to thank him and his wife Esther for being so generous. But I faced more challenges. As this is a Chinese cookbook, ideally all serving wares used have to be Chinese. My sister was able to bring me some of the supplies from home—my late mother's collection of Chinese bowls, chopsticks, and ceramic wares were put to good use in this book.

Not all pictures in this cookbook were styled or composed the exact way I would love them to, but I had basically tried my best. Some of the props are not Chinese, but I just had to make do with whatever I had on hand.

I am personally quite pleased with what I have produced, but there is always room for improvement. I hope you like what I have presented here and hopefully, every single shot of the finished dish would make your mouth water and tempt you to try the recipe!

Index

The Tuttle Story: "Books to Span the East and West"

Most people are surprised to learn that the world's largest publisher of books on Asia had its beginnings in the tiny American state of Vermont. The company's founder, Charles E. Tuttle, belonged to a New England family steeped in publishing. And his first love was naturally books—especially old and rare editions.

Immediately after WW II, serving in Tokyo under General Douglas MacArthur, Tuttle was tasked with reviving the Japanese publishing industry, and founded the Charles E. Tuttle Publishing Company, which thrives today as one of the world's leading independent publishers.

Though a westerner, Charles was hugely instrumental in bringing knowledge of Japan and Asia to a world hungry for information about the East. By the time of his death in 1993, Tuttle had published over 6,000 books on Asian culture, history and art—a legacy honored by the Japanese emperor with the "Order of the Sacred Treasure," the highest tribute Japan can bestow upon a non-Japanese.

With a backlist of 1,500 titles, Tuttle Publishing is more active today than at any time in its past—inspired by Charles' core mission to publish fine books to span the East and West and provide a greater understanding of each.

Published by Tuttle Publishing, an imprint of Periplus Editions (HK) Ltd.

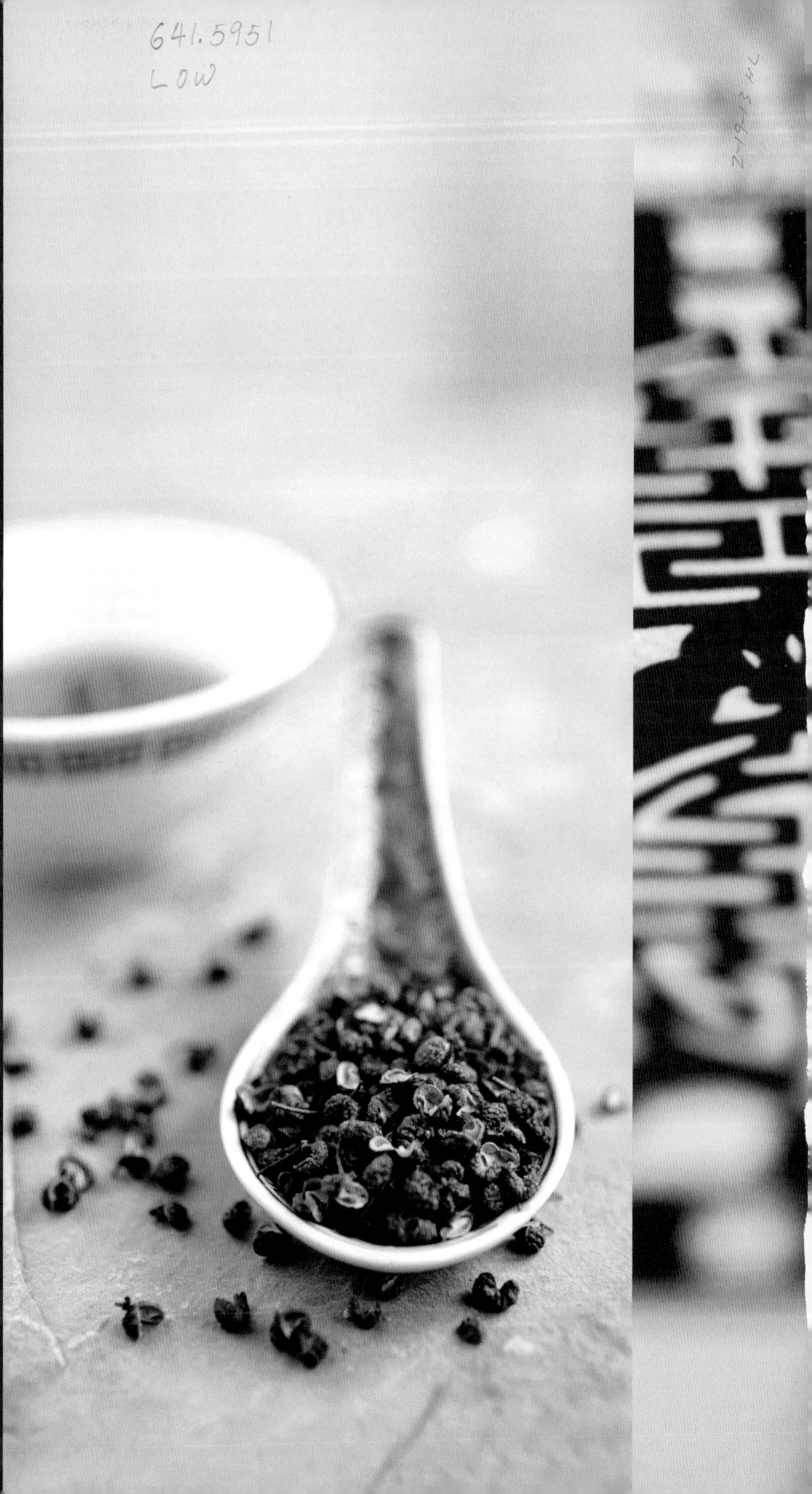

www.tuttlepublishing.com

Library of Congress Cataloging-in-Publication Data

Low, Bee Yinn.
Easy Chinese Recipes : Family Favorites from Dim Sum to Kung Pao / Bee Yinn Low ; foreword by Jaden Hair. -- 1st ed.
p. cm.
Includes index.
ISBN 978-0-8048-4147-4 (hardcover)
1. Cooking, Chinese. 2. Cookbooks. I. Title.
TX724.5.C5L679 2011
641.5951--dc22
2010051700

ISBN 978-0-8048-4147-4

Distributed by

North America, Latin America & Europe
Tuttle Publishing
364 Innovation Drive
North Clarendon, VT 05759-9436 U.S.A.
Tel: 1 (802) 773-8930; Fax: 1 (802) 773-6993
info@tuttlepublishing.com
www.tuttlepublishing.com

Japan
Tuttle Publishing
Yaekari Building, 3rd Floor
5-4-12 Osaki; Shinagawa-ku; Tokyo 141-0032
Tel: (81) 3 5437-0171; Fax: (81) 3 5437-0755
sales@tuttle.co.jp
www.tuttle.co.jp

Asia Pacific
Berkeley Books Pte. Ltd.
61 Tai Seng Avenue, #02-12
Singapore 534167
Tel: (65) 6280-1330; Fax: (65) 6280-6290
inquiries@periplus.com.sg
www.periplus.com

15 14 13 12
10 9 8 7 6 5 4 3 2

Printed in Singapore 1201CP

TUTTLE PUBLISHING® is a registered trademark of Tuttle Publishing, a division of Periplus Editions (HK) Ltd.